Third Edition

GREAT
JOBS

FOR

English
Majors

Julie DeGalan & Stephen Lambert

McGraw·Hill

New York   Chicago   San Francisco   Lisbon   London   Madrid   Mexico City
Milan   New Delhi   San Juan   Seoul   Singapore   Sydney   Toronto

1 2 3 4 5 6 7 8 9 0   DOC/DOC   0 9 8 7 6

ISBN 0-07-145875-1

McGraw-Hill books are available at special quantity discounts to use as premiums and sales
promotions, or for use in corporate training programs. For more information, please write to the
Director of Special Sales, Professional Publishing, McGraw-Hill, Two Penn Plaza, New York, NY 10121-
2298. Or contact your local bookstore.

This book is printed on acid-free paper.

To Joyce and Rip. Thank you for showing me how to learn.
I'll never forget our dinner conversations and hearing you say,
"Fetch the dictionary!"

TM

Contents

Acknowledgments

Writing the third edition of *Great Jobs for English Majors* provided a great opportunity to make a variety of updates and add new information for the reader.

We want to thank our colleagues at McGraw-Hill who were so helpful and patient with us. Monica Bentley and Nancy Hall, we appreciate all your assistance and patience!

We also want to thank Barbra Alan, Rebecca Stevens, and Marsi Wisniewski for checking website addresses and endless other information for us. Your hard work is deeply appreciated.

Introduction

English: A Degree for Every Decade

Sometime, if you can, stop by your college or university library to see whether it holds a collection of yearbooks from the past. Perhaps they are put away for safekeeping in a special collection. Ask to see them and flip through the galleries of past graduates. Begin in the 1960s and enjoy yourself as you look at the conservative haircuts and clothes. Note, too, how mature most of these students look, and reflect on how much less of a transition it must have been for them to pass, at least in appearance, from the world of college to the world of work.

Students of the past mimicked older adults in dress, manners, and behavior. Their closets and drawers were filled with a wardrobe that, with little change, would suffice for most adult occupations. The typical infractions of college rules that warranted discipline tended not to be behavior that rejected adult norms, but rather actions that imitated adults even more closely, such as smoking or drinking.

A Degree with a History

Of course, you'll notice each graduate's degree displayed proudly under his or her photograph. One thing that will immediately be apparent is how many fewer degree options there were. You'll see lots of teacher candidates and lots of science majors. History majors and some foreign language majors appear. But, again and again, you'll see *English* boldly emblazoned under the graduates' serious but youthful mien as they stare out from a page that probably seems far more remote in time than it really is.

This was a time when, if you chose to major in English, people seldom asked, "What are you going to do with that degree?" English was the flagship of the classic undergraduate liberal arts education, and its value lay in its broad exposure to the sweep and history of a culture that spoke and wrote in English. It was valued because of its history as one of the earliest degrees in the middle-class American college tradition, as well as for its emphasis on the disciplines of learning to read, write, and appreciate literature in many forms.

The English majors whose faces appear in yearbooks of the past became leaders in banking, finance, business, education, and medicine. Not only did they feel prepared for these roles by their English degrees, but society also agreed with them and valued that degree as excellent career preparation for a host of possible employment situations.

English Majors Caught in Transition

Now, move through time and take a look at some yearbooks from the end of the 1970s and the early 1980s. Things were quite different for these students; there was an active rebellion against the norms of their parents' generation. The hairstyles and clothes you see in these photos are a dead giveaway of a rejection of traditional norms.

Changes were also taking place in degree programs as students sought out more esoteric majors and many seemed to delight in pursuing studies for which there seemed to be no immediate transferability to the world of work. Students were disaffected with society's power base, and rather than become part of it and manage change from within, many chose to reject it entirely.

But, in the meantime, the technical revolution was under way. Space flight was becoming a regular occurrence, and computer technology was becoming more important in nearly every sector of the economy. Society was adopting technology at an exponential rate. Everyone agreed that the more technical your background was, the greater your chances of success and your ability to master your environment would be. The press held much of this growth up for public adulation, and parents, interested in a return on their considerable investment in college, urged their sons and daughters to major in specialized technical fields.

Just as colleges and universities began offering new technical degree programs, employers, too, developed a penchant for hiring college grads with these narrowly defined degrees. They began to demand specialized graduates for specialized jobs. They only looked at business graduates or computer science majors or economists. They increased the demand for students who had some narrow skills but who did not read widely, who were not comfortable writing, and who had not been schooled in the critical analysis of ideas.

A Failure in Priorities

Many programs that emphasized technology failed to teach students how to communicate this new technology in a way others could easily understand. They emphasized equipment before logical thinking, clarity of purpose, or the ability to follow through in developing an idea. Exams in these subject areas tended to emphasize the same dimensions of speed, efficiency, and economy of effort as did the subject content; tests were heavily skewed in favor of the true/false or multiple-choice exam. Students did well in selecting the correct response but proved terribly deficient in interviews with prospective employers, in completing graduate school personal essays, and in providing writing samples because they had not had the opportunity to develop their written and verbal communication skills.

Both educators and employers soon realized that what they were gaining in depth in these subject areas, they were losing in breadth. The stage was set for the return of the English major.

A Meaningful Degree for Today

Today's students have to leap a far wider chasm of appearance, behavior, and even idiomatic speech than did students of past decades to attain employment. In the contemporary youth-oriented culture, students (even older students) mimic adolescents in their language, choice of entertainment, and physical appearance. Therefore, after the long-held status of "student" is lost upon graduation from college, inexperienced job candidates must negotiate an unfamiliar terrain of language, behavior norms, and dress codes. Most students sense the enormity of these changes, and this can add to their reluctance to begin the job search.

In today's world, the variety of degrees further obscures the choices for first-year college students. Business concentrations have become specialized, including marketing, advertising, and consumer behavior, all of which have enjoyed enormous growth. Although they may have peaked in popularity, they still compete for students.

Parents' Concerns

Some of this trend to such new subject areas and increasing specialization of study is not the students' choice, but rather a response to their parents' demands. Parents of college-age students tend to be keenly aware of how their own employment prospects have or have not been fulfilled and which of their peers has found success in a career. College places a difficult financial burden on families today, and parents naturally want to ensure a return on their investment in a college education. They have continued to stress new degree choices to their children, and some colleges have responded by creating curriculums around these demands. As a result, the English degree is not often termed "hot."

Employers' Needs

Employers, however, are once again realizing that the English major not only already has an expertise employers need desperately, but also that English majors have, in their academic training, the kind of solid preparation needed to learn the ins and outs of any new environment. The world of work is filled with communications, made both easier and faster through technology. The proliferation of communications has for many firms created a quality crisis. Management now realizes through costly errors that even in this technological era businesses need employees who can use language correctly and effectively.

English as a major is now enjoying another in a continuing series of rediscoveries by both students and employers. This process of constant reevaluation of the English degree is one of the principle reasons it maintains its viability in the curriculum. Its current popularity came about through the failure of other programs to emphasize a bedrock need of the world outside of college: solid, effective communication skills.

Why a Degree in English Is So Important Now

An English major is an educational preparation that works for almost any field of endeavor. Human interaction is all about communication. Whether a person is trying to outline to a computer specialist the kind of database to be constructed or is attempting to convey to an executive caterer the ambiance a business function needs to achieve, he or she must rely on an understanding, appreciation, and mastery of the English language.

Work, be it teaching at a prestigious university or rigging an offshore oil derrick, is about people communicating—explaining, arguing, expostulating, describing, elaborating, defining, agreeing, questioning, probing, clarifying, and even obscuring meaning as we come together to get work done. Regardless of the project at hand, the cost, or the technology involved, almost all projects come down to the exchange of meaning between individuals through language.

The staying power of English as a major is based on its ability to meet our basic need for communication, for clarity, for the exchange of meaning to get our work done correctly, efficiently, and with some degree of harmony. Yes, we forget this need sometimes in our fascination with technology, but eventually we realize that workers who understand and appreciate how to use language—how to make it say what we want, how to refine and demystify it—are urgently needed in today's workplace. This is why the English major will always be a welcome job candidate.

How does the English major acquire this skill with language? What do you study that helps you develop these abilities? Although college English departments vary dramatically and their offerings expand and contract depending on the size of the faculty and student body, we can make several solid generalizations about them.

Most English departments try to provide students with a comprehensive acquaintance with English literature from at least Chaucer's time until our own, and with American literature of the nineteenth and twentieth centuries. You may wonder what relevance Chaucer could possibly have for the modern age. Historians have long said, "If you want to know the future, read history." A study of the English language is a study of ideas, cultures, mores, and concepts through time. We study English to be truly educated, and the English major brings to his or her employment setting a high level of general information about the ideas of people and how those ideas have been expressed.

Chaucer may be the demarcation point for a study of English literature, but the author of *The Canterbury Tales* reappears in this career text as a contemporary technical writer! Six hundred years ago, Geoffrey Chaucer wrote *A Treatise on the Astrolabe*, now recognized as an early and quite competent piece of technical writing. What's more, it has reappeared in scientific journals as a model for infusing technical writing, which is often dense and turgid, with style, grace, and rhetoric. No other anecdote could better prove the point of the resiliency and potential application of an English degree.

English study expands your vocabulary, enriches your idiomatic expressions, and provides you with a never-ending set of alternatives in both verbal and written communications. The writing practice you've received has allowed you to enjoy the challenge of writing, not avoid it. You've grown to appreciate the importance of editing, proofreading, and clarifying written text to ensure the best presentation of your ideas.

Employers hope you'll consider putting these valuable skills to use in their workplace. Your reading skills will be of inestimable aid in mastering the technical jargon of whatever environment you select. You'll find yourself understanding policies and procedures and building a new vocabulary around your workplace. Even advanced technical subjects are not beyond the scope of the well-prepared English major, who can read for content and use a dictionary when needed.

A Degree for Today and the Future

Just as Chaucer has proved remarkably current and long-lived, so will the English degree prove important, versatile, and supremely applicable to life in an ever more complicated world. Other academic subjects may move in and out of favor, but English will continue to maintain its hold on successive generations of students and employers because it prepares students well for life and work in innumerable settings.

Look at some of the issues waiting for English majors in the workplace. An increasing reliance on technology to enhance communication, from voice mail to electronic mail, has left many bemoaning the deterioration of language into shorter and more meaningless "sound bites." A subject of a continuing dialogue in workplaces across the country is the growing schism between techno-language and traditional language. The English major can help establish better norms for electronic communication, demonstrating that condensation of language for reasons of cost or technology does not have to sacrifice clarity, grace, or style.

Hiring a generation of specialists has produced another startlingly embarrassing problem. Communications, even public communications, in the workplace have deteriorated in the quality of their spelling, composition, and syntax. Both internal and external communications are filled with errors that undermine the effectiveness and prestige of an organization and can do serious harm if miscommunication results. The English majors working in these environments, regardless of their work role, can help to reestablish quality writing through the high standards they maintain in their own writing and the editing and proofreading they contribute to those around them.

Planning what you want to say, outlining main points, providing effective visual aids, and ensuring that what you have to say is of interest to your audience all come naturally to English majors. They understand how to take complex material and make it clear to a wide audience. The opportunity to improve the effectiveness of a sales presentation, the clarity and structure of training and development programs, or the impact of public relations efforts are all fruitful vineyards for the English major who wonders, "What can I bring to the workplace?"

English majors might be surprised that their talents can be both so notice-able and so needed in the workplace. "How bad can it be?" they ask. The situation is quite poor, and many employers continue to insist in interviews and articles that many of their administrative problems would be eased if they could find management staff who have solid writing and speaking competencies.

No one need worry about the future of the English major in colleges and universities. Though its popularity has waxed and waned, it remains a solid choice for good reasons. Other majors may appear on the scene, only to fade as student interest shifts to something else, but English remains because it is timeless, has broad applications, and contains infinite pathways for explo-ration. English connects us through clarity of meaning and expression; it moves us through poetry, drama, and prose; and be it an ancient Valentine card or a high school commencement address, it is the stuff of memory.

PART ONE

THE JOB SEARCH

1

The Self-Assessment

Self-assessment is the process by which you begin to acknowledge your own particular blend of education, experiences, values, needs, and goals. It provides the foundation for career planning and the entire job search process. Self-assessment involves looking inward and asking yourself what can sometimes prove to be difficult questions. This self-examination should lead to an intimate understanding of your personal traits and values, consumption patterns and economic needs, longer-term goals, skill base, preferred skills, and underdeveloped skills.

You come to the self-assessment process knowing yourself well in some of these areas, but you may still be uncertain about other aspects. You may be well aware of your consumption patterns, but have you spent much time specifically identifying your longer-term goals or your personal values as they relate to work? No matter what level of self-assessment you have undertaken to date, it is now time to clarify all of these issues and questions as they relate to the job search.

The knowledge you gain in the self-assessment process will guide the rest of your job search. In this book, you will learn about all of the following tasks:

- Writing résumés and cover letters
- Researching careers and networking
- Interviewing and job offer considerations

In each of these steps, you will rely on and often return to the understanding gained through your self-assessment. Any individual seeking employment must be able and willing to express these facets of his or her personality to recruiters and interviewers throughout the job search. This communication allows you to show the world who you are so that together with employers you can determine whether there will be a workable match with a given job or career path.

How to Conduct a Self-Assessment

The self-assessment process goes on naturally all the time. People ask you to clarify what you mean, you make a purchasing decision, or you begin a new relationship. You react to the world and the world reacts to you. How you understand these interactions and any changes you might make because of them are part of the natural process of self-discovery. There is, however, a more comprehensive and efficient way to approach self-assessment with regard to employment.

Because self-assessment can become a complex exercise, we have distilled it into a seven-step process that provides an effective basis for undertaking a job search. The seven steps include the following:

1. Understanding your personal traits
2. Identifying your personal values
3. Calculating your economic needs
4. Exploring your longer-term goals
5. Enumerating your skill base
6. Recognizing your preferred skills
7. Assessing skills needing further development

As you work through your self-assessment, you might want to create a worksheet similar to the one shown in Exhibit 1.1, starting on the following page. Or you might want to keep a journal of the thoughts you have as you undergo this process. There will be many opportunities to revise your self-assessment as you start down the path of seeking a career.

Step 1   Understand Your Personal Traits
Each person has a unique personality that he or she brings to the job search process. Gaining a better understanding of your personal traits can help you evaluate job and career choices. Identifying these traits and then finding employment that allows you to draw on at least some of them can create a rewarding and fulfilling work experience. If potential employment doesn't allow you to use these preferred traits, it is important to decide whether you

Exhibit 1.1
SELF-ASSESSMENT WORKSHEET

Step 1. Understand Your Personal Traits
The personal traits that describe me are
(Include all of the words that describe you.)
The ten personal traits that most accurately describe me are
(List these ten traits.)

Step 2. Identify Your Personal Values
Working conditions that are important to me include
(List working conditions that would have to exist for you to accept a position.)
The values that go along with my working conditions are
(Write down the values that correspond to each working condition.)
Some additional values I've decided to include are
(List those values you identify as you conduct this job search.)

Step 3. Calculate Your Economic Needs
My estimated minimum annual salary requirement is
(Write the salary you have calculated based on your budget.)
Starting salaries for the positions I'm considering are
(List the name of each job you are considering and the associated starting salary.)

Step 4. Explore Your Longer-Term Goals
My thoughts on longer-term goals right now are
(Jot down some of your longer-term goals as you know them right now.)

Step 5. Enumerate Your Skill Base
The general skills I possess are
(List the skills that underlie tasks you are able to complete.)
The specific skills I possess are
(List more technical or specific skills that you possess, and indicate your level of expertise.)
General and specific skills that I want to promote to employers for the jobs I'm considering are
(List general and specific skills for each type of job you are considering.)

continued

Step 6. Recognize Your Preferred Skills

Skills that I would like to use on the job include

(List skills that you hope to use on the job, and indicate how often you'd like to use them.)

Step 7. Assess Skills Needing Further Development

Some skills that I'll need to acquire for the jobs I'm considering include

(Write down skills listed in job advertisements or job descriptions that you don't currently possess.)

I believe I can build these skills by

(Describe how you plan to acquire these skills.)

---

can find other ways to express them or whether you would be better off not considering this type of job. Interests and hobbies pursued outside of work hours can be one way to use personal traits you don't have an opportunity to draw on in your work. For example, if you consider yourself an outgoing person and the kinds of jobs you are examining allow little contact with other people, you may be able to achieve the level of interaction that is comfortable for you outside of your work setting. If such a compromise seems impractical or otherwise unsatisfactory, you probably should explore only jobs that provide the interaction you want and need on the job.

Many young adults who are not very confident about their employability will downplay their need for income. They will say, "Money is not all that important if I love my work." But if you begin to document exactly what you need for housing, transportation, insurance, clothing, food, and utilities, you will begin to understand that some jobs cannot meet your financial needs and it doesn't matter how wonderful the job is. If you have to worry each payday about bills and other financial obligations, you won't be very effective on the job. Begin now to be honest with yourself about your needs.

Begin the self-assessment process by creating an inventory of your personal traits. Make a list of as many words as possible to describe yourself. Words like *accurate, creative, future-oriented, relaxed,* or *structured* are just a few examples. In addition, you might ask people who know you well how they might describe you.

Focus on Selected Personal Traits. Of all the traits you identified, select the ten you believe most accurately describe you. Keep track of these ten traits.

Consider Your Personal Traits in the Job Search Process. As you begin exploring jobs and careers, watch for matches between your personal traits and the job descriptions you read. Some jobs will require many personal traits you know you possess, and others will not seem to match those traits.

Working as a public relations information officer, for example, requires nearly nonstop communication with other members of the organization and with external constituents, and the ability to think on your feet and make quick decisions about how to respond to a wide variety of questions. Information officers must exude self-confidence and have an outgoing personality, the ability to express thoughts clearly and simply, and a good sense of humor. A writer's work, on the other hand, is often solitary and requires self-discipline, motivation, curiosity, and observation.

Your ability to respond to changing conditions, your decision-making ability, productivity, creativity, and verbal skills all have a bearing on your success in and enjoyment of your work life. To better guarantee success, be sure to take the time needed to understand these traits in yourself.

Step 2 Identify Your Personal Values

Your personal values affect every aspect of your life, including employment, and they develop and change as you move through life. Values can be defined as principles that we hold in high regard, qualities that are important and desirable to us. Some values aren't ordinarily connected to work (love, beauty, color, light, relationships, family, or religion), and others are (autonomy, cooperation, effectiveness, achievement, knowledge, and security). Our values determine, in part, the level of satisfaction we feel in a particular job.

Define Acceptable Working Conditions. One facet of employment is the set of working conditions that must exist for someone to consider taking a job.

Each of us would probably create a unique list of acceptable working conditions, but items that might be included on many people's lists are the amount of money you would need to be paid, how far you are willing to drive or travel, the amount of freedom you want in determining your own schedule, whether you would be working with people or data or things, and the types of tasks you would be willing to do. Your conditions might include statements of working conditions you will *not* accept; for example, you might not be willing to work at night or on weekends or holidays.

If you were offered a job tomorrow, what conditions would have to exist for you to realistically consider accepting the position? Take some time and make a list of these conditions.

Realize Associated Values. Your list of working conditions can be used to create an inventory of your values relating to jobs and careers you are exploring. For example, if one of your conditions stated that you wanted to earn at least $30,000 per year, the associated value would be financial gain. If another condition was that you wanted to work with a friendly group of people, the value that went along with that might be belonging or interaction with people.

Relate Your Values to the World of Work. As you read the job descriptions you come across either in this book, in newspapers and magazines, or online, think about the values associated with each position.

For example, the duties of an English teacher include developing course content based on an established curriculum, presenting course material in meaningful ways for all types of learners, grading assignments, and inspiring attention and commitment to the material. Associated values are communication, effectiveness, creativity, and organization.

At least some of the associated values in the field you're exploring should match those you extracted from your list of working conditions. Take a second look at any values that don't match up. How important are they to you? What will happen if they are not satisfied on the job? Can you incorporate those personal values elsewhere? Your answers need to be brutally honest. As you continue your exploration, be sure to add to your list any additional values that occur to you.

Step 3 Calculate Your Economic Needs

Each of us grew up in an environment that provided for certain basic needs, such as food and shelter, and, to varying degrees, other needs that we now consider basic, such as cable television, e-mail, or an automobile. Needs such as privacy, space, and quiet, which at first glance may not appear to be monetary needs, may add to housing expenses and so should be considered as you examine your economic needs. For example, if you place a high value on a large, open living space for yourself, it would be difficult to satisfy that need without an associated high housing cost, especially in a densely populated city environment.

As you prepare to move into the world of work and become responsible for meeting your own basic needs, it is important to consider the salary you will need to be able to afford a satisfying standard of living. The three-step process outlined here will help you plan a budget, which in turn will allow you to evaluate the various career choices and geographic locations you are considering. The steps include (1) develop a realistic budget, (2) examine starting salaries, and (3) use a cost-of-living index.

Develop a Realistic Budget. Each of us has certain expectations for the kind of lifestyle we want to maintain. To begin the process of defining your economic needs, it will be helpful to determine what you expect to spend on routine monthly expenses. These expenses include housing, food, transportation, entertainment, utilities, loan repayments, and revolving charge accounts. You may not currently spend anything for certain items, but you probably will have to once you begin supporting yourself. As you develop this budget, be generous in your estimates, but keep in mind any items that could be reduced or eliminated. If you are not sure about the cost of a certain item, talk with family or friends who would be able to give you a realistic estimate.

If this is new or difficult for you, start to keep a log of expenses right now. You may be surprised at how much you actually spend each month for food or stamps or magazines. Household expenses and personal grooming items can often loom very large in a budget, as can auto repairs or home maintenance.

Income taxes must also be taken into consideration when examining salary requirements. State and local taxes vary, so it is difficult to calculate exactly the effect of taxes on the amount of income you need to generate. To roughly estimate the gross income necessary to generate your minimum annual salary requirement, multiply the minimum salary you have calculated by a factor of 1.35. The resulting figure will be an approximation of what your gross income would need to be, given your estimated expenses.

Examine Starting Salaries. Starting salaries for each of the career tracks are provided throughout this book. These salary figures can be used in conjunction with the cost-of-living index (discussed in the next section) to determine whether you would be able to meet your basic economic needs in a given geographic location.

Use a Cost-of-Living Index. If you are thinking about trying to get a job in a geographic region other than the one where you now live, understanding differences in the cost of living will help you come to a more informed decision about making a move. By using a cost-of-living index, you can compare salaries offered and the cost of living in different locations with what you know about the salaries offered and the cost of living in your present location.

Many variables are used to calculate the cost-of-living index. Often included are housing, groceries, utilities, transportation, health care, clothing, and entertainment expenses. Right now you do not need to worry about the details associated with calculating a given index. The main purpose of this exercise is to help you understand that pay ranges for entry-level positions may not vary greatly, but the cost of living in different locations *can* vary tremendously.

Let's say you want to find a job as an advertising coordinator in a large metropolitan community and you currently live in Columbus, Ohio. According to information contained on the American Society for Training and Development website (http://astd.salary .com), an advertising coordinator's salary varies according to geographic location. As of the publication date, the estimated average beginning advertising coordinator salaries in Columbus and two other cities were $37,780 in Burlington, Vermont, $38,633 in Phoenix, and $39,099 in Columbus.

Although the average beginning salary is highest in Columbus, if you will be relocating to either of the other cities you need to take into account the cost of living in each place to fully understand the impact of the salary you would earn there. For example, a comparison of the living expenses in Burlington and Columbus indicates that you would need to make $43,366 in Burlington to maintain the same purchasing power as you would have with a $39,099 salary in Columbus. So if you moved to Burlington from Columbus you would receive a lower salary and have a higher cost of living (see the following list), so you would experience a loss of almost $5,600 in disposable income.

Groceries are 4 percent higher in Burlington
Housing is about the same cost

Utilities are 20 percent higher in Burlington
Transportation is about the same cost
Health care is 25 percent higher in Burlington
Miscellaneous goods/services are 17 percent higher in
Burlington

If a change in an advertising coordinator position involved moving from Columbus to Phoenix, you would need to earn $39,515 in Phoenix to have the same purchasing power as in Columbus—the cost of living in Phoenix is about 1 percent higher than in Columbus. Remember, the average beginning advertising coordinator salary in Phoenix is $38,633, so the lower salary would mean a loss of about $900 in disposable income. The cost-of-living comparison shows:

Groceries are about the same in the two locations
Housing is 10 percent higher in Phoenix
Utilities are 18 percent higher in Columbus
Transportation is 8 percent higher in Phoenix
Health care is 24 percent higher in Phoenix
Miscellaneous goods/services are 7 percent higher in
Phoenix

You also need to evaluate whether an opportunity for employment that involves relocating to a different geographic location will advance your career or meet personal needs. Other cities may have more opportunities for advancement, but you need to make sure that relocating will be financially feasible.

You can work through a similar exercise for any type of job you are considering and for many locations when current salary information is available. It will be worth your time to undertake this analysis if you are seriously considering a relocation. By doing so you will be able to make an informed choice.

Step 4 Explore Your Longer-Term Goals

There is no question that when we first begin working, our goals are to use our skills and education in a job that will reward us with employment, income, and status relative to the preparation we brought with us to this position. If we are not being paid as much as we feel we should for our level of education or if job demands don't provide the intellectual stimulation we had hoped for, we experience unhappiness and as a result often seek other employment.

Most jobs we consider "good" are those that fulfill our basic "lower-level" needs of security, food, clothing, shelter, income, and productive work. But even when our basic needs are met and our jobs are secure and productive, we as individuals are constantly changing. As we change, the demands and expectations we place on our jobs may change. Fortunately, some jobs grow and change with us, and this explains why some people are happy throughout many years in a job.

But more often people are bigger than the jobs they fill. We have more goals and needs than any job could satisfy. These are "higher-level" needs of self-esteem, companionship, affection, and an increasing desire to feel we are employing ourselves in the most effective way possible. Not all of these higher-level needs can be met through employment, but for as long as we are employed, we increasingly demand that our jobs play their part in moving us along the path to fulfillment.

Another obvious but important fact is that we change as we mature. Although our jobs also have the potential for change, they may not change as frequently or as markedly as we do. There are increasingly fewer one-job, one-employer careers; we must think about a work future that may involve voluntary or forced moves from employer to employer. Because of that very real possibility, we need to take advantage of the opportunities in each position we hold. Acquiring the skills and competencies associated with each position will keep us viable and attractive as employees. This is particularly true in a job market that not only is technology/computer dependent, but also is populated with more and more small, self-transforming organizations rather than the large, seemingly stable organizations of the past.

If you are considering a career in college admissions in higher education, you would gain a solid understanding of this path if you talked to an entry-level admissions representative, a director of college admissions, and, finally, someone who has risen through the ranks and now serves as the university's vice president of student affairs. Each will have unique perspectives, concerns, and value priorities.

Step 5   Enumerate Your Skill Base

In terms of the job search, skills can be thought of as capabilities that can be developed in school, at work, or by volunteering and then used in specific job settings. Many studies have documented the kinds of skills that employers seek in entry-level applicants. For example, some of the most desired skills for individuals interested in the teaching profession are the ability to interact effectively with students one-on-one, to manage a classroom, to adapt to varying situations as necessary, and to get involved in school activities. Business employers have also identified important qualities, including enthusiasm for the employer's product or service, a businesslike mind, the ability to follow written or oral instructions, the ability to demonstrate self-control, the confidence to suggest new ideas, the ability to communicate with all members of a group, an awareness of cultural differences, and loyalty, to name just a few. You will find that many of these skills are also in the repertoire of qualities demanded in your college major.

To be successful in obtaining any given job, you must be able to demonstrate that you possess a certain mix of skills that will allow you to carry out the duties required by that job. This skill mix will vary a great deal from job to job; to determine the skills necessary for the jobs you are seeking, you can read job advertisements or more generic job descriptions, such as those found later in this book. If you want to be effective in the job search, you must directly show employers that you possess the skills needed to be successful in filling the position. These skills will initially be described on your résumé and then discussed again during the interview process.

Skills are either general or specific. To develop a list of skills relevant to employers, you must first identify the general skills you possess, then list specific skills you have to offer, and, finally, examine which of these skills employers are seeking.

Identify Your General Skills. Because you possess or will possess a college degree, employers will assume that you can read and write, perform certain basic computations, think critically, and communicate effectively. Employers will want to see that you have acquired these skills, and they will want to know which additional general skills you possess.

One way to begin identifying skills is to write an experiential diary. An experiential diary lists all the tasks you were responsible for completing for each job you've held and then outlines the skills required to do those tasks. You may list several skills for any given task. This diary allows you to distinguish between the tasks you performed and the underlying skills required to complete those tasks. Here's an example:

Tasks	Skills
Answering telephone	Effective use of language, clear diction, ability to direct inquiries, ability to solve problems
Waiting on tables	Poise under conditions of time and pressure, speed, accuracy, good memory, simultaneous completion of tasks, sales skills

For each job or experience you have participated in, develop a worksheet based on the example shown here. On a résumé, you may want to describe these skills rather than simply listing tasks. Skills are easier for the employer to appreciate, especially when your experience is very different from the employment you are seeking. In addition to helping you identify general skills, this experiential diary will prepare you to speak more effectively in an interview about the qualifications you possess.

Identify Your Specific Skills. It may be easier to identify your specific skills because you can definitely say whether you can speak other languages, program a computer, draft a map or diagram, or edit a document using appropriate symbols and terminology.

Using your experiential diary, identify the points in your history where you learned how to do something very specific, and decide whether you have a beginning, intermediate, or advanced knowledge of how to use that particular skill. Right now, be sure to list *every* specific skill you have, and don't consider whether you like using the skill. Write down a list of specific skills you have acquired and the level of competence you possess—beginning, intermediate, or advanced.

Relate Your Skills to Employers. You probably have thought about a couple of different jobs you might be interested in obtaining, and one way to begin relating the general and specific skills you possess to a potential employer's needs is to read actual advertisements for these types of positions (see Part Two for resources listing actual job openings).

For example, you might be interested in working as a brand manager. A typical entry-level assistant brand manager job listing might read, "Provide support to brand managers. Interact daily with members of a cross-functional team and with external vendors. Requires bachelor's degree with one year experience." If you then use any one of a number of general sources of information that describe the job of brand manager, you would find additional information. Assistant brand managers also help design new packaging, identify new product opportunities, and research current dynamics in the marketplace.

Begin building a comprehensive list of required skills with the first job description you read. Exploring online job advertisements of several related positions will reveal an important core of skills that is necessary for obtaining the type of work you're interested in. In building this list, include both general and specific skills.

The following is a sample list of skills needed to be successful as an assistant brand manager. These items were extracted from both general resources and actual job listings.

JOB: ASSISTANT BRAND MANAGER

General Skills	Specific Skills
Attention to detail	Manage marketing project budgets
Analytical approach to problem solving	Develop new product marketing strategies
Project management	Manage iterative design process
Creativity	Develop new product names
Organizational skills	Coordinate artwork development, photography, and printing

Try to generate a comprehensive list of required skills for at least one job you are considering.

The list of general skills that you develop for a given career path will be valuable for any number of jobs. Many of the specific skills would also be transferable to other types of positions. For example, managing a project budget is a required skill for

some assistant brand managers, and it also would be required of
some media planners as well.

___

Step 6   Recognize Your Preferred Skills

In the previous section you developed a comprehensive list of skills that
relate to particular career paths that are of interest to you. You can now relate
these to skills that you prefer to use. We all use a wide range of skills (some
researchers say individuals have a repertoire of about five hundred skills), but
we may not particularly be interested in using all of them in our work. There
may be some skills that come to us more naturally or that we use successfully time and time again and that we want to continue to use; these are best
described as our preferred skills. For this exercise use the list of skills that
you created for the previous section, and decide which of them you are *most
interested in using* in future work and how often you would like to use them.
You might be interested in using some skills only occasionally, while others
you would like to use more regularly. You probably also have skills that you
hope you can use constantly.

As you examine job announcements, look for matches between this list of
preferred skills and the qualifications described in the advertisements. These
skills should be highlighted on your résumé and discussed in job interviews.

Step 7   Assess Skills Needing Further Development

Previously you compiled a list of general and specific skills required for given
positions. You already possess some of these skills; those that remain to be
developed are your underdeveloped skills.

If you are just beginning the job search, there may be gaps between the
qualifications required for some of the jobs you're considering and the skills
you possess. The thought of having to admit to and talk about these underdeveloped skills, especially in a job interview, is a frightening one. One way
to put a healthy perspective on this subject is to target and relate your explo-
ration of underdeveloped skills to the types of positions you are seeking. Recognizing these shortcomings and planning to overcome them with either
on-the-job training or additional formal education can be a positive way to
address the concept of underdeveloped skills.

On your worksheet or in your journal, make a list of up to five general
or specific skills required for the positions you're interested in that you *don't
currently possess*. For each item list an idea you have for specific action you
could take to acquire that skill. Do some brainstorming to come up with
possible actions. If you have a hard time generating ideas, talk to people cur-

rently working in this type of position, professionals in your college career services office, trusted friends, family members, or members of related professional associations.

In the chapter on interviewing, we will discuss in detail how to effectively address questions about underdeveloped skills. Generally speaking, though, employers want genuine answers to these types of questions. They want you to reveal "the real you," and they also want to see how you answer difficult questions. In taking the positive, targeted approach discussed previously, you show the employer that you are willing to continue to learn and that you have a plan for strengthening your job qualifications.

Use Your Self-Assessment

Exploring entry-level career options can be an exciting experience if you have good resources available and will take the time to use them. Can you effectively complete the following tasks?

1. Understand your personality traits and relate them to career choices
2. Define your personal values
3. Determine your economic needs
4. Explore longer-term goals
5. Understand your skill base
6. Recognize your preferred skills
7. Express a willingness to improve on your underdeveloped skills

If so, then you can more meaningfully participate in the job search process by writing a more effective résumé, finding job titles that represent work you are interested in doing, locating job sites that will provide the opportunity for you to use your strengths and skills, networking in an informed way, participating in focused interviews, getting the most out of follow-up contacts, and evaluating job offers to find those that create a good match between you and the employer. The remaining chapters in Part One guide you through these next steps in the job search process. For many job seekers, this process can take anywhere from three months to a year to implement. The time you will need to put into your job search will depend on the type of job you want and the geographic location where you'd like to work. Think of your effort as a job in itself, requiring you to set aside time each week to complete the needed work. Carefully undertaken efforts may reduce the time you need for your job search.

The Résumé and
Cover Letter

The task of writing a résumé may seem overwhelming if you are unfamiliar with this type of document, but there are some easily understood techniques that can and should be used. This section was written to help you understand the purpose of the résumé, the different types of formats available, and how to write the sections that contain information traditionally found on a résumé. We will present examples and explanations that address questions frequently posed by people writing their first résumé or updating an old one.

Even within the formats and suggestions given, however, there are infinite variations. True, most follow one of the outlines suggested, but you should feel free to adjust the résumé to suit your needs and make it expressive of your life and experience.

Why Write a Résumé?

The purpose of a résumé is to convince an employer that you should be interviewed. Whether you're mailing, faxing, or e-mailing this document, you'll want to present enough information to show that you can make an immediate and valuable contribution to an organization. A résumé is not an indepth historical or legal document; later in the job search process you may be asked to document your entire work history on an application form and attest to its validity. The résumé should, instead, highlight relevant information pertaining directly to the organization that will receive the document or to the type of position you are seeking.

We will discuss the chronological and digital résumés in detail here. Functional and targeted résumés, which are used much less often, are briefly discussed. The reasons for using one type of résumé over another and the typical format for each are addressed in the following sections.

The Chronological Résumé

The chronological résumé is the most common of the various résumé formats and therefore the format that employers are most used to receiving. This type of résumé is easy to read and understand because it details the chronological progression of jobs you have held. (See Exhibit 2.1.) It begins with your most recent employment and works back in time. If you have a solid work history or have experience that provided growth and development in your duties and responsibilities, a chronological résumé will highlight these achievements. The typical elements of a chronological résumé include the heading, a career objective, educational background, employment experience, activities, and references.

The Heading
The heading consists of your name, address, telephone number, and other means of contact. This may include a fax number, e-mail address, and your home-page address. If you are using a shared e-mail account or a parent's business fax, be sure to let others who use these systems know that you may receive important professional correspondence via these systems. You wouldn't want to miss a vital e-mail or fax! Likewise, if your résumé directs readers to a personal home page on the Web, be certain it's a professional personal home page designed to be viewed and appreciated by a prospective employer. This may mean making substantial changes in the home page you currently mount on the Web.

The Objective
Without a doubt the objective statement is the most challenging part of the résumé for most writers. Even for individuals who have decided on a career path, it can be difficult to encapsulate all they want to say in one or two brief sentences. For job seekers who are unfocused or unclear about their intentions, trying to write this section can inhibit the entire résumé writing process.

Keep the objective as short as possible and no longer than two short sentences.

Exhibit 2.1
CHRONOLOGICAL RÉSUMÉ

BEAU B. HAYS

Student Apartment 36
University of Maryland
College Park, MD 20742
(301) 405-1212
bbhays@xxx.net
(until May 2007)

555 Potomac Street
Hagerstown, MD 21740
(301) 555-1212
beaubhays@xxx.net

OBJECTIVE

Entry-level position as a technical writer for a management consulting firm.

EDUCATION

Bachelor of Arts in English Language and Literature
University of Maryland, College Park, MD
May 2007

EXPERIENCE

Intern, Accenture (consulting management firm), Virginia Office, Jan. 2007–
  Present.
Work as an off-site technical writer on projects involving global positioning
  systems (GPS). Develop draft explanatory text for various types of reports
  used by corporations in a variety of industries.

Sales Associate, REI, College Park, MD, Sept. 2005–Jan. 2007.
Answered questions about GPS units for sale, determined best product for
  customers based on how they would use the GPS. Interfaced with GPS
  manufacturers to obtain information requested by customers.

Reporter, Diamondback (campus newspaper), University of Maryland, College
  Park, MD, Sept. 2005–Dec. 2006.
Developed and wrote stories for the "Diversions" section of the paper:
  student organization activities, movie reviews, campus lectures, and
  other events.

continued

ACTIVITIES
Terrapin Trail Club, active member, three years
English Department Writing Center volunteer, two years
Intramural baseball, one year

REFERENCES
Excellent professional references available upon request.

Choose one of the following types of objective statement:

1. General Objective Statement

• An entry-level educational programming coordinator position

2. Position-Focused Objective

• To obtain the position of conference coordinator at State College

3. Industry-Focused Objective

• To begin a career as a sales representative in the cruise line industry

4. Summary of Qualifications Statement

A degree in English Language and Literature and three years of growing job responsibility at a bank have prepared me to begin a career as a writer with a federal monetary agency that values accuracy, attention to detail, and proficiency in a range of relevant software.

Support Your Objective. A résumé that contains any one of these types of objective statements should then go on to demonstrate why you are qualified to get the position. Listing academic degrees can be one way to indicate qualifications. Another demonstration would be in the way previous experiences, both volunteer and paid, are described. Without this kind of documentation in the body of the résumé, the objective looks unsupported.

Think of the résumé as telling a connected story about you. All the elements should work together to form a coherent picture that ideally should relate to your statement of objective.

Education

This section of your résumé should indicate the exact name of the degree you will receive or have received, spelled out completely with no abbreviations. The degree is generally listed after the objective, followed by the institution name and location, and then the month and year of graduation. This section could also include your academic minor, grade point average (GPA), and appearance on the Dean's List or President's List.

If you have enough space, you might want to include a section listing courses related to the field in which you are seeking work. The best use of a "related courses" section would be to list some course work that is not traditionally associated with the major. Perhaps you took several computer courses outside your degree that will be helpful and related to the job prospects you are entertaining. Several education section examples are shown here:

- Bachelor of Arts in English; Emphasis in Communications; Adams State College, Alamosa, Colorado; May 2007
- Bachelor of Arts Degree in English; Alabama State University, Montgomery, Alabama; December 2007; Minor: Communications
- Bachelor of Arts Degree in English; Whitworth College, Spokane, Washington; May 2007

An example of a format for a related courses section follows:

RELATED COURSES

Desktop Publishing	Advanced Composition
Writing for Mass Media	Journalism
Technical Writing	Organizational Communications

Experience

The experience section of your résumé should be the most substantial part and should take up most of the space on the page. Employers want to see what kind of work history you have. They will look at your range of experiences, longevity in jobs, and specific tasks you are able to complete. This section may also be called "work experience," "related experience," "employment history," or "employment." No matter what you call this section, some important points to remember are the following:

1. **Describe your duties** as they relate to the position you are seeking.
2. **Emphasize major responsibilities** and indicate increases in responsibility. Include all relevant employment experiences: summer, part-time, internships, cooperative education, or self-employment.
3. **Emphasize skills**, especially those that transfer from one situation to another. The fact that you coordinated a student organization, chaired meetings, supervised others, and managed a budget leads one to suspect that you could coordinate other things as well.
4. **Use descriptive job titles** that provide information about what you did. A "Student Intern" should be more specifically stated as, for example, "Magazine Operations Intern." "Volunteer" is also too general; a title such as "Peer Writing Tutor" would be more appropriate.
5. **Create word pictures** by using active verbs to start sentences. Describe *results* you have produced in the work you have done.

A limp description would say something such as the following: "My duties included helping with production, proofreading, and editing. I used a design and page layout program." An action statement would be stated as follows: "Coordinated and assisted in the creative marketing of brochures and seminar promotions, becoming proficient in Quark."

Remember, an accomplishment is simply a result, a final measurable product that people can relate to. A duty is not a result; it is an obligation—every job holder has duties. For an effective résumé, list as many results as you can. To make the most of the limited space you have and to give your description impact, carefully select appropriate and accurate descriptors.

Here are some traits that employers tell us they like to see:

- Teamwork
- Energy and motivation
- Learning and using new skills
- Versatility
- Critical thinking
- Understanding how profits are created
- Organizational acumen

- Risk taking
- Communicating directly and clearly, in both writing and speaking
- Willingness to admit mistakes
- High personal standards

Solutions to Frequently Encountered Problems

Repetitive Employment with the Same Employer
EMPLOYMENT: The Foot Locker, Portland, Oregon. Summer 2001, 2002, 2003. Initially employed in high school as salesclerk. Because of successful performance, asked to return next two summers at higher pay with added responsibility. Ranked as the #2 salesperson the first summer and #1 the next two summers. Assisted in arranging eye-catching retail displays; served as manager of other summer workers during owner's absence.

A Large Number of Jobs
EMPLOYMENT: Recent Hospitality Industry Experience: Affiliated with four upscale hotel/restaurant complexes (September 2001–February 2004), where I worked part- and full-time as a waiter, bartender, disc jockey, and bookkeeper to produce income for college.

Several Positions with the Same Employer
EMPLOYMENT: Coca-Cola Bottling Co., Burlington, Vermont, 2001–2004. In four years, I received three promotions, each with increased pay and responsibility.

Summer Sales Coordinator: Promoted to hire, train, and direct efforts of add-on staff of fifteen college-age route salespeople hired to meet summer peak demand for product.

Sales Administrator: Promoted to run home office sales desk, managing accounts and associated delivery schedules for professional sales force of ten people. Intensive phone work, daily interaction with all personnel, and strong knowledge of product line required.

Route Salesperson: Summer employment to travel and tourism industry sites that use Coke products. Met specific schedule demands, used good communication skills with wide variety of customers, and demonstrated strong selling skills. Named salesperson of the month for July and August of that year.

Questions Résumé Writers Often Ask

How Far Back Should I Go in Terms of Listing Past Jobs?

Usually, listing three or four jobs should suffice. If you did something back in high school that has a bearing on your future aspirations for employment, by all means list the job. As you progress through your college career, high school jobs will be replaced on the résumé by college employment.

Should I Differentiate Between Paid and Nonpaid Employment?

Most employers are not initially concerned about how much you were paid. They are eager to know how much responsibility you held in your past employment. There is no need to specify that your work was as a volunteer if you had significant responsibilities.

How Should I Represent My Accomplishments or Work-Related Responsibilities?

Succinctly, but fully. In other words, give the employer enough information to arouse curiosity but not so much detail that you leave nothing to the imagination. Besides, some jobs merit more lengthy explanations than others. Be sure to convey any information that can give an employer a better understanding of the depth of your involvement at work. Did you supervise others? How many? Did your efforts result in a more efficient operation? How much did you increase efficiency? Did you handle a budget? How much? Were you promoted in a short time? Did you work two jobs at once or fifteen hours per week after high school? Where appropriate, quantify.

Should the Work Section Always Follow the Education Section on the Résumé?

Always lead with your strengths. If your education closely relates to the employment you now seek, put this section after the objective. If your education does not closely relate but you have a surplus of good work experiences, consider reversing the order of your sections to lead with employment, followed by education.

How Should I Present My Activities, Honors, Awards, Professional Societies, and Affiliations?

This section of the résumé can add valuable information for an employer to consider if used correctly. The rule of thumb for information in this section is to include only those activities that are in some way relevant to the objective stated on your résumé. If you can draw a valid connection between your activities and your objective, include them; if not, leave them out.

Professional affiliations and honors should all be listed; especially important are those related to your job objective. Social clubs and activities need not be a part of your résumé unless you hold a significant office or you are looking for a position related to your membership. Be aware that most prospective employers' principal concerns are related to your employability, not your social life. If you have any, publications can be included as an addendum to your résumé.

How Should I Handle References?

The use of references is considered a part of the interview process, and they should never be listed on a résumé. You would always provide references to a potential employer if requested to, so it is not even necessary to include this section on the résumé if space does not permit. If space is available, it is acceptable to include the following statement:

- References furnished upon request.

The Functional Résumé

A functional résumé departs from a chronological résumé in that it organizes information by specific accomplishments in various settings: previous jobs, volunteer work, associations, and so forth. This type of résumé permits you to stress the substance of your experiences rather than the position titles you have held. You should consider using a functional résumé if you have held a series of similar jobs that relied on the same skills or abilities. There are many good books in which you can find examples of functional résumés, including *How to Write a Winning Resume* or *Resumes Made Easy*.

The Targeted Résumé

The targeted résumé focuses on specific work-related capabilities you can bring to a given position within an organization. Past achievements are listed to highlight your capabilities and the work history section is abbreviated.

Digital Résumés

Today's employers have to manage an enormous number of résumés. One of the most frequent complaints the writers of this series hear from students is the failure of employers to even acknowledge the receipt of a résumé and cover letter. Frequently, the reason for this poor response or nonresponse is the volume of applications received for every job. In an attempt to better manage the considerable labor investment involved in processing large numbers of résumés, many employers are requiring digital submission of résumés. There are two types of digital résumés: those that can be e-mailed or posted to a website, called *electronic résumés*, and those that can be "read" by a computer, commonly called *scannable résumés*. Though the format may be a bit different from the traditional "paper" résumé, the goal of both types of digital résumés is the same—to get you an interview! These résumés must be designed to be "technologically friendly." What that basically means to you is that they should be free of graphics and fancy formatting. (See Exhibit 2.2.)

Electronic Résumés

Sometimes referred to as plain-text résumés, electronic résumés are designed to be e-mailed to an employer or posted to one of many commercial Internet databases such as Careerbuilder.com, America's Job Bank (ajb.dni.us), or Monster.com.

Some technical considerations:

- Electronic résumés must be written in American Standard Code for Information Interchange (ASCII), which is simply a plain-text format. These characters are universally recognized so that every computer can accurately read and understand them. To create an ASCII file of your current résumé, open your document, then save it as a text or ASCII file. This will eliminate all formatting. Edit as needed using your computer's text editor application.
- Use a standard-width typeface. Courier is a good choice because it is the font associated with ASCII in most systems.
- Use a font size of 11 to 14 points. A 12-point font is considered standard.
- Your margin should be left-justified.
- Do not exceed sixty-five characters per line because the word-wrap function doesn't operate in ASCII.

Exhibit 2.2
DIGITAL RÉSUMÉ

BEAU B. HAYS ◄──────────────────── Put your name at the
Student Apartment 36   top on its own line.
University of Maryland
College Park, MD 20742
301-405-1212 ◄──────────────────────── Put your phone number
bbhays@xxx.net   on its own line.

KEYWORD SUMMARY ◄
Professional writing   Keywords make your
Management consulting   résumé easier to find in
Technical writing   a database.
Global positioning system
GPS

OBJECTIVE
Entry-level position as a technical writer for a   Use a standard-width
management consulting firm.   typeface.

EDUCATION
Bachelor of Arts in English Language and Literature
University of Maryland, College Park, MD, May 2007

EXPERIENCE
Intern, Accenture (consulting management firm),
Virginia Office, January 2007 - Present.
* Work as off-site technical writer.   Use a space between
* Draft explanatory text for various types of reports.   asterisk and text.
* Focus on use of Global Positioning Systems.

Sales Associate, REI,   No line should exceed
College Park, MD, September 2005 - January 2007.   sixty-five characters.
* Answered customer questions about GPS units.
* Determined most appropriate unit for each customer.
* Interfaced with GPS manufacturers.
* Conveyed manufacturer's information to customers.

continued

Reporter, Diamondback campus paper, University of Maryland,
College Park, MD, September 2005 - December 2006.
* Developed story ideas for "Diversions" section.
* Attended campus events.
* Wrote descriptive stories and reviews.
* Assisted with office duties.

ACTIVITIES ◄—————————————————— Capitalize letters to
emphasize headings.
* Terrapin Trail Club, active member 3 years
* English Department Writing Center, volunteer, 2 years
* Intramural baseball, 1 year   End each line by
hitting the ENTER
(or RETURN) key.
REFERENCES
Excellent professional references available upon request.

- Do not use boldface, italics, underlining, bullets, or various font sizes. Instead, use asterisks, plus signs, or all capital letters when you want to emphasize something.
- Avoid graphics and shading.
- Use as many "keywords" as you possibly can. These are words or phrases usually relating to skills or experience that either are specifically used in the job announcement or are popular buzzwords in the industry.
- Minimize abbreviations.
- Your name should be the first line of text.
- Conduct a "test run" by e-mailing your résumé to yourself and a friend before you send it to the employer. See how it transmits, and make any changes you need to. Continue to test it until it's exactly how you want it to look.
- Unless an employer specifically requests that you send the résumé in the form of an attachment, don't. Employers can encounter problems opening a document as an attachment, and there are always viruses to consider.
- Don't forget your cover letter. Send it along with your résumé as a single message.

Scannable Résumés

Some companies are relying on technology to narrow the candidate pool for available job openings. Electronic Applicant Tracking uses imaging to scan, sort, and store résumé elements in a database. Then, through OCR (Optical Character Recognition) software, the computer scans the résumés for keywords and phrases. To have the best chance at getting an interview, you want to increase the number of "hits"—matches of your skills, abilities, experience, and education to those the computer is scanning for—your résumé will get. You can see how critical using the right keywords is for this type of résumé.

Technical considerations include:

- Again, do not use boldface (newer systems may be able to read this, but many older ones won't), italics, underlining, bullets, shading, graphics, or multiple font sizes. Instead, for emphasis, use asterisks, plus signs, or all capital letters. Minimize abbreviations.
- Use a popular typeface such as Courier, Helvetica, Arial, or Palatino. Avoid decorative fonts.
- Font size should be between 11 and 14 points.
- Do not compress the spacing between letters.
- Use horizontal and vertical lines sparingly; the computer may misread them as the letters *L* or *I*.
- Left-justify the text.
- Do not use parentheses or brackets around telephone numbers, and be sure your phone number is on its own line of text.
- Your name should be the first line of text and on its own line. If your résumé is longer than one page, be sure to put your name on the top of all pages.
- Use a traditional résumé structure. The chronological format may work best.
- Use nouns that are skill-focused, such as *management*, *writer*, and *programming*. This is different from traditional paper résumés, which use action-oriented verbs.
- Laser printers produce the finest copies. Avoid dot-matrix printers.
- Use standard, light-colored paper with text on one side only. Since the higher the contrast, the better, your best choice is black ink on white paper.
- Do not staple or fold your résumé. This can confuse the computer.

- Always send original copies. If you must fax, set the fax on fine mode, not standard.
- Before you send your scannable résumé, be certain the employer uses this technology. If you can't determine this, you may want to send two versions (scannable and traditional) to be sure your résumé gets considered.

Résumé Production and Other Tips

An ink-jet printer is the preferred option for printing your résumé. Begin by printing just a few copies. You may find a small error or you may simply want to make some changes, and it is less frustrating and less expensive if you print in small batches.

Résumé paper color should be carefully chosen. You should consider the types of employers who will receive your résumé and the types of positions for which you are applying. Use white or ivory paper for traditional or conservative employers or for higher-level positions.

Black ink on sharp, white paper can be harsh on the reader's eyes. Think about an ivory or cream paper that will provide less contrast and be easier to read. Pink, green, and blue tints should generally be avoided.

Many résumé writers buy packages of matching envelopes and cover sheet stationery that, although not absolutely necessary, help convey a professional impression.

If you'll be producing many cover letters at home, be sure you have high-quality printing equipment. Learn standard envelope formats for business, and retain a copy of every cover letter you send out. You can use the copies to take notes of any telephone conversations that may occur.

If attending a job fair, either carry a briefcase or place your résumé in a nicely covered legal-size pad holder.

The Cover Letter

The cover letter provides you with the opportunity to tailor your résumé by telling the prospective employer how you can be a benefit to the organization. It allows you to highlight aspects of your background that are not already discussed in your résumé and that might be especially relevant to the organization you are contacting or to the position you are seeking. Every résumé should have a cover letter enclosed when you send it out. Unlike the résumé, which may be mass-produced, a cover letter is most effective when it is individually prepared and focused on the particular requirements of the organization in question.

A good cover letter should supplement the résumé and motivate the reader to review the résumé. The format shown in Exhibit 2.3 (see page 34) is only a suggestion to help you decide what information to include in a cover letter.

Begin the cover letter with your street address six lines down from the top. Leave three to five lines between the date and the name of the person to whom you are addressing the cover letter. Make sure you leave one blank line between the salutation and the body of the letter and between paragraphs. After typing "Sincerely," leave four blank lines and type your name. This should leave plenty of room for your signature. A sample cover letter is shown in Exhibit 2.4 on page 35.

The following guidelines will help you write good cover letters:

1. Be sure to type your letter neatly; ensure there are no misspellings.
2. Avoid unusual typefaces, such as script.
3. Address the letter to an individual, using the person's name and title. To obtain this information, call the company. If answering a blind newspaper advertisement, address the letter "To Whom It May Concern" or omit the salutation.
4. Be sure your cover letter directly indicates the position you are applying for and tells why you are qualified to fill it.
5. Send the original letter, not a photocopy, with your résumé. Keep a copy for your records.
6. Make your cover letter no more than one page.
7. Include a phone number where you can be reached.
8. Avoid trite language and have someone read the letter over to react to its tone, content, and mechanics.
9. For your own information, record the date you send out each letter and résumé.

Exhibit 2.3
COVER LETTER FORMAT

Your Street Address
Your Town, State, Zip
Phone Number
Fax Number
Date   E-mail

Name
Title
Organization
Address

Dear _____ :

First Paragraph. In this paragraph state the reason for the letter, name the specific position or type of work you are applying for, and indicate from which resource (career services office, website, newspaper, contact, employment service) you learned of this opening. The first paragraph can also be used to inquire about future openings.

Second Paragraph. Indicate why you are interested in this position, the company, or its products or services and what you can do for the employer. If you are a recent graduate, explain how your academic background makes you a qualified candidate. Try not to repeat the same information found in the résumé.

Third Paragraph. Refer the reader to the enclosed résumé for more detailed information.

Fourth Paragraph. In this paragraph say what you will do to follow up on your letter. For example, state that you will call by a certain date to set up an interview or to find out if the company will be recruiting in your area. Finish by indicating your willingness to answer any questions the recipient may have. Be sure you have provided your phone number.

Sincerely,

Type your name

Enclosure

Exhibit 2.4
SAMPLE COVER LETTER

555 Potomac Street
Hagerstown, MD 21740
(301) 555-1212
beaubhays@xxx.net

Date

Andrea Phillips
Director of Human Resources
Fifth Avenue Management Consultants, LLC
123 Fifth Avenue
New York, NY 10003

Dear Ms. Phillips:

I read of your opening for a technical writer on Fifth Avenue Management Consultants' website, and I am very interested in talking with you about this position. In May of 2007 I will graduate from the University of Maryland with a bachelor of arts degree in English Language and Literature.

The job description indicates that you are looking for an entry-level technical writer and that a bachelor's degree in English or a related field is required. My degree and work experience may be of interest to you. Most recently, I completed a half-year internship at an international management consulting firm, Accenture. This experience introduced me to the demands placed on a technical writer in a complex organization, which I found to be both challenging and rewarding. In a previous job I worked as a reporter for a large campus newspaper, writing articles that were then critiqued by my student colleagues and the faculty advisor.

The enclosed résumé outlines my education and provides more detail about my related work experience.

I hope to meet with you to discuss how my education and experience are consistent with your needs, and how I could become a valued member of Fifth Avenue Management Consultants' team. Next week I will contact you to

continued

arrange an interview. In the meantime, if you require additional information, please contact me using the telephone number or e-mail address listed above.

Sincerely,

Beau B. Hays

Enclosure

3

Researching Careers and Networking

One reason for confusion is perhaps a mistaken assumption that a college education provides job training. In most cases it does not. Of course, applied fields such as engineering, management, or education provide specific skills for the workplace as well as an education.

What Do They Call the Job You Want?

Your overall college education exposes you to numerous fields of study and teaches you quantitative reasoning, critical thinking, writing, and speaking, all of which can be successfully applied to a number of different job fields. But it still remains up to you to choose a job field and to learn how to articulate the benefits of your education in a way the employer will appreciate.

"What can I really do with my degree?" English majors are much more likely to pose this question than students earning teaching, accounting, and management information systems degrees, just to name a few, because they have not been taught how to begin their careers. Your friend who's an accounting major knows she'll most likely start her career with an accounting firm. Or your friend who's a marketing major is planning to go into sales. If you are not sure what kind of work you are qualified for, or the type of employer that would hire you, this chapter will help you gain that understanding.

Collect Job Titles

The world of employment is a complex place, so you need to become a bit of an explorer and adventurer and be willing to try a variety of techniques to develop a list of possible occupations that might use your talents and education. You might find computerized interest inventories, reference books and other sources, and classified ads helpful in this respect. Once you have a list of possibilities that you are interested in and qualified for, you can move on to find out what kinds of organizations have these job titles.

Computerized Interest Inventories. One way to begin collecting job titles is to identify a number of jobs that call for your degree and the particular skills and interests you identified as part of the self-assessment process. There are excellent interactive career-guidance programs on the market to help you produce such selected lists of possible job titles. Most of these are available at colleges and at some larger town and city libraries. Two of the industry leaders are *CHOICES* and *DISCOVER.* Both allow you to enter interests, values, educational background, and other information to produce lists of possible occupations and industries. Each of the resources listed here will produce different job title lists. Some job titles will appear again and again, while others will be unique to a particular source. Investigate all of them!

Reference Sources. Books on the market that may be available through your local library or career counseling office also suggest various occupations related to specific majors. The following are only a few of the many good books on the market: *College Majors and Careers: A Resource Guide for Effective Life Planning* by Paul Phifer, *Guide to College Majors* by Erik Olson and Lisa M. Rovito, and *College Majors Handbook with Real Career Paths and Payoffs* by Paul Harrington and Thomas Harrington. All of these books list possible job titles within the academic major.

As you begin exploring the types of employers that hire English majors interested in, say, technical writing, you will begin to see that some seem like a better fit than others. Technical writers work in major corporations selling either consumer or industrial goods, in medical institutions, in financial organizations, or in small venture capital start-up companies that produce specialized computer software.

Each employer offers a different environment or "culture" with associated norms in the pace of work, in the formality of communications, in office attire, and the background and training of those you'll be working alongside. Do any of the following types of employers seem more interesting to you: nonprofit agency, federal government agency, county education department, private school, state government agency, or international corporation? As with job titles, look for work environments that are more attractive to you.

Each job title deserves your consideration. Like removing the layers of an onion, the search for job titles can go on and on! As you spend time doing this activity, you are actually learning more about the value of your degree. What's important in your search at this point is not to become critical or selective but rather to develop as long a list of possibilities as you can. Every source used will help you add new and potentially exciting jobs to your growing list.

Classified Ads. It has been well publicized that the classified ad section of the newspaper represents only a small fraction of the current job market. Nevertheless, the weekly classified ads can be a great help to you in your search. Although they may not be the best place to look for a job, they can teach you a lot about the job market. Classified ads provide a good education in job descriptions, duties, responsibilities, and qualifications. In addition, they provide insight into which industries are actively recruiting and some indication of the area's employment market. This is particularly helpful when seeking a position in a specific geographic area and/or a specific field. For your purposes, classified ads are a good source for job titles to add to your list.

Read the Sunday classified ads in a major market newspaper for several weeks in a row. Cut and paste all the ads that interest you and seem to call for something close to your education, skills, experience, and interests. Remember that classified ads are written for what an organization *hopes* to find; you don't have to meet absolutely every criterion. However, if certain requirements are stated as absolute minimums and you cannot meet them, it's best not to waste your time and that of the employer.

The weekly classified want ads exercise is important because these jobs are out in the marketplace. They truly exist, and people with your qualifications are being sought to apply. What's more, many of these advertisements describe the duties and responsibilities of the job advertised and give you a beginning sense of the challenges and opportunities such a position presents. Some will indicate salary, and that will be helpful as well. This information will better define the jobs for you and provide some good material for possible interviews in that field.

Explore Job Descriptions

Once you've arrived at a solid list of possible job titles that interest you and for which you believe you are somewhat qualified, it's a good idea to do some research on each of these jobs. The preeminent source for such job information is the *Dictionary of Occupational Titles*, or *DOT* (http://online.onet center.org). This directory lists every conceivable job and provides excellent up-to-date information on duties and responsibilities, interactions with associates, and day-to-day assignments and tasks. These descriptions provide a thorough job analysis, but they do not consider the possible employers or the environments in which a job may be performed. So, although a position as public relations officer may be well defined in terms of duties and responsibilities, it does not explain the differences in doing public relations work in a college or a hospital or a factory or a bank. You will need to look somewhere else for work settings.

Learn More About Possible Work Settings

After reading some job descriptions, you may choose to edit and revise your list of job titles once again, discarding those you feel are not suitable and keeping those that continue to hold your interest. Or you may wish to keep your list intact and see where these jobs may be located. For example, if you are interested in public relations and you appear to have those skills and the requisite education, you'll want to know which organizations do public relations. How can you find that out? How much income does someone in public relations make a year and what is the employment potential for the field of public relations?

To answer these and many other questions about your list of job titles, we recommend you try any of the following resources: *Careers Encyclopedia*, the professional societies and resources found throughout this book, *College to Career: The Guide to Job Opportunities*, and the *Occupational Outlook Handbook* (http://stats.bls.gov/ocohome.htm). Each of these resources, in a different way, will help to put the job titles you have selected into an employer context. Perhaps the most extensive discussion is found in the *Occupational Outlook Handbook*, which gives a thorough presentation of the nature of the work, the working conditions, employment statistics, training, other qualifications, and advancement possibilities as well as job outlook and earnings. Related occupations are also detailed, and a select bibliography is provided to help you find additional information.

Continuing with our public relations example, your search through these reference materials would teach you that the public relations jobs you find attractive are available in larger hospitals, financial institutions, most corporations (both consumer goods and industrial goods), media organizations, and colleges and universities.

Networking

Networking is the process of deliberately establishing relationships to get career-related information or to alert potential employers that you are available for work. Networking is critically important to today's job seeker for two reasons: it will help you get the information you need, and it can help you find out about *all* of the available jobs.

Get the Information You Need

Networkers will review your résumé and give you feedback on its effectiveness. They will talk about the job you are looking for and give you a candid appraisal of how they see your strengths and weaknesses. If they have a good sense of the industry or the employment sector for that job, you'll get their feelings on future trends in the industry as well. Some networkers will be very forthcoming about salaries, job-hunting techniques, and suggestions for your job search strategy. Many have been known to place calls right from the interview desk to friends and associates who might be interested in you. Each networker will make his or her own contribution, and each will be valuable.

Because organizations must evolve to adapt to current global market needs, the information provided by decision makers within various organizations will be critical to your success as a new job market entrant. For example, you might learn about the concept of virtual organizations from a networker. Virtual organizations coordinate economic activity to deliver value to customers by using resources outside the traditional boundaries of the organization. This concept is being discussed and implemented by chief executive officers of many organizations, including Ford Motor, Dell, and IBM. Networking can help you find out about this and other trends currently affecting the industries under your consideration.

Find Out About All of the Available Jobs

Not every job that is available at this very moment is advertised for potential applicants to see. This is called the *hidden job market*. Only 15 to 20 percent of all jobs are formally advertised, which means that 80 to 85 percent of available jobs do not appear in published channels. Networking will help you become more knowledgeable about all the employment opportunities available during your job search period.

Although someone you might talk to today doesn't know of any openings within his or her organization, tomorrow or next week or next month an opening may occur. If you've taken the time to show an interest in and knowledge of their organization, if you've shown the company representative how you can help achieve organizational goals and that you can fit into the organization, you'll be one of the first candidates considered for the position.

Networking: A Proactive Approach
Networking is a proactive rather than a reactive approach. You, as a job seeker, are expected to initiate a certain level of activity on your own behalf; you cannot afford to simply respond to jobs listed in the newspaper. Being proactive means building a network of contacts that includes informed and interested decision makers who will provide you with up-to-date knowledge of the current job market and increase your chances of finding out about employment opportunities appropriate for your interests, experience, and level of education. An old axiom of networking says, "You are only two phone calls away from the information you need." In other words, by talking to enough people, you will quickly come across someone who can offer you help.

Preparing to Network

In deliberately establishing relationships, maximize your efforts by organizing your approach. Five specific areas in which you can organize your efforts include reviewing your self-assessment, reviewing your research on job sites and organizations, deciding who you want to talk to, keeping track of all your efforts, and creating your self-promotion tools.

Review Your Self-Assessment
Your self-assessment is as important a tool in preparing to network as it has been in other aspects of your job search. You have carefully evaluated your personal traits, personal values, economic needs, longer-term goals, skill base, preferred skills, and underdeveloped skills. During the networking process you will be called upon to communicate what you know about yourself and

relate it to the information or job you seek. Be sure to review the exercises that you completed in the self-assessment section of this book in preparation for networking. We've explained that you need to assess which skills you have acquired from your major that are of general value to an employer; be ready to express those in ways he or she can appreciate as useful in the organizations.

Review Research on Job Sites and Organizations

In addition, individuals assisting you will expect that you'll have at least some background information on the occupation or industry of interest to you. Refer to the appropriate sections of this book and other relevant publications to acquire the background information necessary for effective networking. They'll explain how to identify not only the job titles that might be of interest to you but also which kinds of organizations employ people to do that job. You will develop some sense of working conditions and expectations about duties and responsibilities—all of which will be of help in your networking interviews.

Decide Who You Want to Talk To

Networking cannot begin until you decide who you want to talk to and, in general, what type of information you hope to gain from your contacts. Once you know this, it's time to begin developing a list of contacts. Five useful sources for locating contacts are described here.

College Alumni Network. Most colleges and universities have created a formal network of alumni and friends of the institution who are particularly interested in helping currently enrolled students and graduates of their alma mater gain employment-related information.

It is usually a simple process to make use of an alumni network. Visit your college's website and locate the alumni office and/or your career center. Either or both sites will have information about your school's alumni network. You'll be provided with information on shadowing experiences, geographic information, or those alumni offering job referrals. If you don't find what you're looking for, don't hesitate to phone or e-mail your career center and ask what they can do to help you connect with an alum.

Alumni networkers may provide some combination of the following services: day-long shadowing experiences, telephone interviews, in-person interviews, information on relocating to given geographic areas, internship information, suggestions on graduate school study, and job vacancy notices.

Present and Former Supervisors. If you believe you are on good terms with present or former job supervisors, they may be an excellent resource for providing information or directing you to appropriate resources that would have information related to your current interests and needs. Additionally, these supervisors probably belong to professional organizations that they might be willing to utilize to get information for you.

Employers in Your Area. Although you may be interested in working in a geographic location different from the one where you currently reside, don't overlook the value of the knowledge and contacts those around you are able to provide. Use the local telephone directory and newspaper to identify the types of organizations you are thinking of working for or professionals who have the kinds of jobs you are interested in. Recently, a call made to a local hospital's financial administrator for information on working in health-care financial administration yielded more pertinent information on training seminars, regional professional organizations, and potential employment sites than a national organization was willing to provide.

Employers in Geographic Areas Where You Hope to Work. If you are thinking about relocating, identifying prospective employers or informational contacts in the new location will be critical to your success. Here are some tips for online searching. First, use a "metasearch" engine to get the most out of your search. Metasearch engines combine several engines into one powerful tool. We frequently use dogpile.com and metasearch.com for this purpose. Try using the city and state as your keywords in a search. *New Haven, Connecticut* will bring you to the city's website with links to the chamber of commerce, member businesses, and other valuable resources. By using looksmart.com you can locate newspapers in any area, and they, too, can provide valuable insight before you relocate. Of course, both dogpile and metasearch can lead you to yellow and white page directories in areas you are considering.

Professional Associations and Organizations. Professional associations and organizations can provide valuable information in several areas: career paths that you might not have considered, qualifications relating to those career choices, publications that list current job openings, and workshops or seminars that will enhance your professional knowledge and skills. They can also be excellent sources for background information on given industries: their health, current problems, and future challenges.

There are several excellent resources available to help you locate professional associations and organizations that would have information to meet your needs. Two especially useful publications are the *Encyclopedia of Associations* and *National Trade and Professional Associations of the United States*.

Keep Track of All Your Efforts

It can be difficult, almost impossible, to remember all the details related to each contact you make during the networking process, so you will want to develop a record-keeping system that works for you. Formalize this process by using your computer to keep a record of the people and organizations you want to contact. You can simply record the contact's name, address, and telephone number, and what information you hope to gain.

You could record this as a simple Word document and you could still use the "Find" function if you were trying to locate some data and could only recall the firm's name or the contact's name. If you're comfortable with database management and you have some database software on your computer, then you can put information at your fingertips even if you have only the zip code! The point here is not technological sophistication but good record keeping.

Once you have created this initial list, it will be helpful to keep more detailed information as you begin to actually make the contacts. Those details should include complete contact information, the date and content of each contact, names and information for additional networkers, and required follow-up. Don't forget to send a letter thanking your contact for his or her time! Your contact will appreciate your recall of details of your meetings and conversations, and the information will help you to focus your networking efforts.

Create Your Self-Promotion Tools

There are two types of promotional tools that are used in the networking process. The first is a résumé and cover letter, and the second is a one-minute "infomercial," which may be given over the telephone or in person.

Techniques for writing an effective résumé and cover letter are discussed in Chapter 2. Once you have reviewed that material and prepared these important documents, you will have created one of your self-promotion tools.

The one-minute infomercial will demand that you begin tying your interests, abilities, and skills to the people or organizations you want to network with. Think about your goal for making the contact to help you understand what you should say about yourself. You should be able to express yourself easily and convincingly. If, for example, you are contacting an alumnus of your institution to obtain the names of possible employment sites in a distant city, be prepared to discuss why you are interested in moving to that location, the types of jobs you are interested in, and the skills and abilities you possess that will make you a qualified candidate.

To create a meaningful one-minute infomercial, write it out, practice it as if it will be a spoken presentation, rewrite it, and practice it again if necessary until expressing yourself comes easily and is convincing.

Here's a simplified example of an infomercial for use over the telephone:

Hello, Mrs. Jones? My name is Beau Hays. I am a recent graduate of the University of Maryland, and I hope to pursue a career in technical writing. My major was English, and I feel I've developed entry-level skills that would be valued by an employer. I'm an active listener, a critical thinker, and a clear and concise writer. I'm also familiar with a variety of word-processing software.

Mrs. Jones, I'm calling you because I still need more information about working as a technical writer, and one of my professors recommended that I talk with you. I'm hoping you'll have time to meet with me for about half an hour to discuss your perspective on this type of writing career. There are so many types of jobs and employers, and I'm seeking advice on the options that would be the best fit for my combination of skills and experience.

Would you be willing to meet with me? I am available any afternoon after one o'clock, if that would work for you.

It very well may happen that your employer contact wishes you to communicate by e-mail. The infomercial quoted above could easily be rewritten for an e-mail message. You should "cut and paste" your résumé right into the e-mail text itself.

Other effective self-promotion tools include portfolios for those in the arts, writing professions, or teaching. Portfolios show examples of work, photographs of projects or classroom activities, or certificates and credentials that are job related. There may not be an opportunity to use the portfolio during an interview, and it is not something that should be left with the organization. It is designed to be explained and displayed by the creator. However, during some networking meetings, there may be an opportunity to illustrate a point or strengthen a qualification by exhibiting the portfolio.

Beginning the Networking Process

Set the Tone for Your Communications

It can be useful to establish "tone words" for any communications you embark upon. Before making your first telephone call or writing your first letter, decide what you want the person to think of you. If you are networking to try to obtain a job, your tone words might include descriptors such as *genuine, informed,* and *self-knowledgeable.* When you're trying to acquire information, your tone words may have a slightly different focus, such as *courteous, organized, focused,* and *well-spoken.* Use the tone words you establish for your contacts to guide you through the networking process.

Honestly Express Your Intentions

When contacting individuals, it is important to be honest about your reasons for making the contact. Establish your purpose in your own mind and be able and ready to articulate it concisely. Determine an initial agenda, whether it be informational questioning or self-promotion, present it to your contact, and be ready to respond immediately. If you don't adequately prepare before initiating your overture, you may find yourself at a disadvantage if you're asked to immediately begin your informational interview or self-promotion during the first phone conversation or visit.

Start Networking Within Your Circle of Confidence

Once you have organized your approach—by utilizing specific researching methods, creating a system for keeping track of the people you will contact, and developing effective self-promotion tools—you are ready to begin networking. The best way to begin networking is by talking with a group of people you trust and feel comfortable with. This group is usually made up of your family, friends, and career counselors. No matter who is in this inner circle, they will have a special interest in seeing you succeed in your job search. In addition, because they will be easy to talk to, you should try taking some risks in terms of practicing your information-seeking approach. Gain confidence in talking about the strengths you bring to an organization and the underdeveloped skills you feel hinder your candidacy. Be sure to review the section on self-assessment for tips on approaching each of these areas. Ask for critical but constructive feedback from the people in your circle of confidence on the letters you write and the one-minute infomercial you have developed. Evaluate whether you want to make the changes they suggest, then practice the changes on others within this circle.

Stretch the Boundaries of Your Networking Circle of Confidence

Once you have refined the promotional tools you will use to accomplish your networking goals, you will want to make additional contacts. Because you will not know most of these people, it will be a less comfortable activity to undertake. The practice that you gained with your inner circle of trusted friends should have prepared you to now move outside of that comfort zone.

It is said that any information a person needs is only two phone calls away, but the information cannot be gained until you (1) make a reasonable guess about who might have the information you need and (2) pick up the telephone to make the call. Using your network list that includes alumni, instructors, supervisors, employers, and associations, you can begin preparing your list of questions that will allow you to get the information you need.

Prepare the Questions You Want to Ask

Networkers can provide you with the insider's perspective on any given field and you can ask them questions that you might not want to ask in an interview. For example, you can ask them to describe the more repetitious or mundane parts of the job or ask them for a realistic idea of salary expectations. Be sure to prepare your questions ahead of time so that you are organized and efficient.

Be Prepared to Answer Some Questions

To communicate effectively, you must anticipate questions that will be asked of you by the networkers you contact. Revisit the self-assessment process you undertook and the research you've done so that you can effortlessly respond to questions about your short- and long-term goals and the kinds of jobs you are most interested in pursuing.

General Networking Tips

Make Every Contact Count. Setting the tone for each interaction is critical. Approaches that will help you communicate in an effective way include politeness, being appreciative of time provided to you, and being prepared and thorough. Remember, *everyone* within an organization has a circle of influence, so be prepared to interact effectively with each person you encounter in the networking process, including secretarial and support staff. Many information or job seekers have thwarted their own efforts by being rude to some individuals they encountered as they networked because they made the incorrect assumption that certain persons were unimportant.

Sometimes your contacts may be surprised at their ability to help you. After meeting and talking with you, they might think they have not offered much in the way of help. A day or two later, however, they may make a contact that would be useful to you and refer you to that person.

With Each Contact, Widen Your Circle of Networkers. Always leave an informational interview with the names of at least two more people who can help you get the information or job that you are seeking. Don't be shy about asking for additional contacts; networking is all about increasing the number of people you can interact with to achieve your goals.

Make Your Own Decisions. As you talk with different people and get answers to the questions you pose, you may hear conflicting information or get conflicting suggestions. Your job is to listen to these "experts" and decide what information and which suggestions will help you achieve *your* goals. Only implement those suggestions that you believe will work for you.

Shutting Down Your Network

As you achieve the goals that motivated your networking activity—getting the information you need or the job you want—the time will come to inactivate all or parts of your network. As you do, be sure to tell your primary supporters about your change in status. Call or write to each one of them and give them as many details about your new status as you feel is necessary to maintain a positive relationship.

Because a network takes on a life of its own, activity undertaken on your behalf will continue even after you cease your efforts. As you get calls or are contacted in some fashion, be sure to inform these networkers about your change in status, and thank them for assistance they have provided.

Information on the latest employment trends indicates that workers will change jobs or careers several times in their lifetime. Networking, then, will be a critical aspect in the span of your professional life. If you carefully and thoughtfully conduct your networking activities during your job search, you will have a solid foundation of experience when you need to network the next time around.

Where Are These Jobs, Anyway?

Having a list of job titles that you've designed around your own career interests and skills is an excellent beginning. It means you've really thought about who you are and what you are presenting to the employment market. It has caused you to think seriously about the most appealing environments to work in, and you have identified some employer types that represent these environments.

The research and the thinking that you've done thus far will be used again and again. They will be helpful in writing your résumé and cover letters, in talking about yourself on the telephone to prospective employers, and in answering interview questions.

Now is a good time to begin to narrow the field of job titles and employment sites down to some specific employers to initiate the employment contact.

Find Out Which Employers Hire People Like You

This section will provide tips, techniques, and specific resources for developing an actual list of specific employers that can be used to make contacts. It is only an outline that you must be prepared to tailor to your own particular needs and according to what you bring to the job search. Once again, it is important to communicate with others along the way exactly what you're looking for and what your goals are for the research you're doing. Librarians, employers, career counselors, friends, friends of friends, business contacts, and bookstore staff will all have helpful information on geographically specific and new resources to aid you in locating employers who'll hire you.

Identify Information Resources

Your interview wardrobe and your new résumé might have put a dent in your wallet, but the resources you'll need to pursue your job search are available for free. The categories of information detailed here are not hard to find and are yours for the browsing.

Numerous resources described in this section will help you identify actual employers. Use all of them or any others that you identify as available in your geographic area. As you become experienced in this process, you'll quickly figure out which information sources are helpful and which are not. If you live in a rural area, a well-planned day trip to a major city that includes a college career office, a large college or city library, state and federal employment centers, a chamber of commerce office, and a well-stocked bookstore can produce valuable results.

There are many excellent resources available to help you identify actual job sites. They are categorized into employer directories (usually indexed by product lines and geographic location), geographically based directories (designed to highlight particular cities, regions, or states), career-specific directories (e.g., *Sports MarketPlace*, which lists tens of thousands of firms involved with sports), periodicals and newspapers, targeted job posting publications, and videos. This is by no means meant to be a complete treatment of resources but rather a starting point for identifying useful resources.

Working from the more general references to highly specific resources, we provide a basic list to help you begin your search. Many of these you'll find easily available. In some cases reference librarians and others will suggest even better materials for your particular situation. Start to create your own customized bibliography of job search references.

Geographically Based Directories. The Job Bank series published by Bob Adams, Inc. (aip.com) contains detailed entries on each area's major employers, including business activity, address, phone number, and hiring contact name. Many listings specify educational backgrounds being sought in potential employees. Each volume contains a solid discussion of each city's or state's major employment sectors. Organizations are also indexed by industry. Job Bank volumes are available for the following places: Atlanta, Boston, Chicago, Dallas–Ft. Worth, Denver, Detroit, Florida, Houston, Los Angeles, Minneapolis, New York, Ohio, Philadelphia, San Francisco, Seattle, St. Louis, Washington, D.C., and other cities throughout the Northwest.

National Job Bank (careercity.com) lists employers in every state, along with contact names and commonly hired job categories. Included are many small companies often overlooked by other directories. Companies are also indexed by industry. This publication provides information on educational backgrounds sought and lists company benefits.

Periodicals and Newspapers. Several sources are available to help you locate which journals or magazines carry job advertisements in your field. Other resources help you identify opportunities in other parts of the country.

- *Where the Jobs Are: A Comprehensive Directory of 1200 Journals Listing Career Opportunities*
- *Corptech Fast 5000 Company Locator*
- *National Ad Search* (nationaladsearch.com)
- *The Federal Jobs Digest* (jobsfed.com) and *Federal Career Opportunities*
- *World Chamber of Commerce Directory* (chamberofcommerce.org)

This list is certainly not exhaustive; use it to begin your job search work.

Targeted Job Posting Publications. Although the resources that follow are national in scope, they are either targeted to one medium of contact (telephone), focused on specific types of jobs, or less comprehensive than the sources previously listed.

- Careers.org (careers.org/index.html)
- *The Job Hunter* (jobhunter.com)
- *Current Jobs for Graduates* (graduatejobs.com)
- *Environmental Opportunities* (ecojobs.com)
- *Y National Vacancy List* (ymca.net/employment/ymca_recruiting/jobright.htm)
- *ArtSEARCH*
- *Community Jobs*
- *National Association of Colleges and Employers: Job Choices series*
- *National Association of Colleges and Employers* (jobweb.com)

Videos. You may be one of the many job seekers who likes to get information via a medium other than paper. Many career libraries, public libraries, and career centers in libraries carry an assortment of videos that will help you learn new techniques and get information helpful in the job search.

Locate Information Resources

Throughout these introductory chapters, we have continually referred you to various websites for information on everything from job listings to career information. Using the Web gives you a mobility at your computer that you don't enjoy if you rely solely on books or newspapers or printed journals. Moreover, material on the Web, if the site is maintained, can be the most up-to-date information available.

You'll eventually identify the information resources that work best for you, but make certain you've covered the full range of resources before you begin to rely on a smaller list. Here's a short list of informational sites that many job seekers find helpful:

- Public and college libraries
- College career centers
- Bookstores
- The Internet
- Local and state government personnel offices
- Career/job fairs

Each one of these sites offers a collection of resources that will help you get the information you need.

As you meet and talk with service professionals at all these sites, be sure to let them know what you're doing. Inform them of your job search, what you've already accomplished, and what you're looking for. The more people who know you're job seeking, the greater the possibility that someone will have information or know someone who can help you along your way.

Interviewing and
Job Offer Considerations

Certainly, there can be no one part of the job search process more fraught with anxiety and worry than the interview. Yet seasoned job seekers welcome the interview and will often say, "Just get me an interview and I'm on my way!" They understand that the interview is crucial to the hiring process and equally crucial for them, as job candidates, to have the opportunity of a personal dialogue to add to what the employer may already have learned from the résumé, cover letter, and telephone conversations.

Believe it or not, the interview is to be welcomed, and even enjoyed! It is a perfect opportunity for you, the candidate, to sit down with an employer and express yourself and display who you are and what you want. Of course, it takes thought and planning and a little strategy; after all, it *is* a job interview! But it can be a positive, if not pleasant, experience and one you can look back on and feel confident about your performance and effort.

For many new job seekers, a job, any job, seems a wonderful thing. But seasoned interview veterans know that the job interview is an important step for both sides—the employer and the candidate—to see what each has to offer and whether there is going to be a "fit" of personalities, work styles, and attitudes. And it is this concept of balance in the interview, that both sides have important parts to play, that holds the key to success in mastering this aspect of the job search strategy.

Try to think of the interview as a conversation between two interested and equal partners. You both have important, even vital, information to deliver and to learn. Of course, there's no denying the employer has some leverage, especially in the initial interview for recruitment or any interview scheduled by the candidate and not the recruiter. That should not prevent the interviewee from seeking to play an equal part in what should be a fair exchange of information. Too often the untutored candidate allows the interview to become one-sided. The employer asks all the questions and the candidate simply responds. The ideal would be for two mutually interested parties to sit down and discuss possibilities for each. This is a conversation of significance, and it requires preparation, thought about the tone of the interview, and planning of the nature and details of the information to be exchanged.

Preparing for the Interview

The length of most initial interviews is about thirty minutes. Given the brevity, the information that is exchanged ought to be important. The candidate should be delivering material that the employer cannot discover on the résumé, and in turn, the candidate should be learning things about the employer that he or she could not otherwise find out. After all, if you have only thirty minutes, why waste time on information that is already published? The information exchanged is more than just factual, and both sides will learn much from what they see of each other, as well. How the candidate looks, speaks, and acts are important to the employer. The employer's attention to the interview and awareness of the candidate's résumé, the setting, and the quality of information presented are important to the candidate.

Just as the employer has every right to be disappointed when a prospect is late for the interview, looks unkempt, and seems ill-prepared to answer fairly standard questions, the candidate may be disappointed with an interviewer who isn't ready for the meeting, hasn't learned the basic résumé facts, and is constantly interrupted by telephone calls. In either situation there's good reason to feel let down.

There are many elements to a successful interview, and some of them are not easy to describe or prepare for. Sometimes there is just a chemistry between interviewer and interviewee that brings out the best in both, and a good exchange takes place. But there is much the candidate can do to pave the way for success in terms of his or her résumé, personal appearance, goals, and interview strategy—each of which we will discuss. However, none of this preparation is as important as the time and thought the candidate gives to personal self-assessment.

Self-Assessment

Neither a stunning résumé nor an expensive, well-tailored suit can compensate for candidates who do not know what they want, where they are going, or why they are interviewing with a particular employer. Self-assessment, the process by which we begin to know and acknowledge our own particular blend of education, experiences, needs, and goals, is not something that can be sorted out the weekend before a major interview. Of all the elements of interview preparation, this one requires the longest lead time and cannot be faked.

Because the time allotted for most interviews is brief, it is all the more important for job candidates to understand and express succinctly why they are there and what they have to offer. This is not a time for undue modesty (or for braggadocio either); it is a time for a compelling, reasoned statement of why you feel that you and this employer might make a good match. It means you have to have thought about your skills, interests, and attributes; related those to your life experiences and your own history of challenges and opportunities; and determined what that indicates about your strengths, preferences, values, and areas needing further development.

If you need some assistance with self-assessment issues, refer to Chapter 1. Included are suggested exercises that can be done as needed, such as making up an experiential diary and extracting obvious strengths and weaknesses from past experiences. These simple assignments will help you look at past activities as collections of tasks with accompanying skills and responsibilities. Don't overlook your high school or college career office. Many offer personal counseling on self-assessment issues and may provide testing instruments such as the *Myers-Briggs Type Indicator (MBTI)*, the *Harrington-O'Shea Career Decision-Making System (CDM)*, the *Strong Interest Inventory (SII)*, or any other of a wide selection of assessment tools that can help you clarify some of these issues prior to the interview stage of your job search.

The Résumé

Résumé preparation has been discussed in detail, and some basic examples were provided. In this section we want to concentrate on how best to use your résumé in the interview. In most cases the employer will have seen the résumé prior to the interview, and, in fact, it may well have been the quality of that résumé that secured the interview opportunity.

An interview is a conversation, however, and not an exercise in reading. So, if the employer hasn't seen your résumé and you have brought it along to the interview, wait until asked or until the end of the interview to offer it. Otherwise, you may find yourself staring at the back of your résumé and simply answering "yes" and "no" to a series of questions drawn from that document.

Sometimes an interviewer is not prepared and does not know or recall the contents of the résumé and may use the résumé to a greater or lesser degree as a "prompt" during the interview. It is for you to judge what that may indicate about the individual performing the interview or the employer. If your interviewer seems surprised by the scheduled meeting, relies on the résumé to an inordinate degree, and seems otherwise unfamiliar with your background, this lack of preparation for the hiring process could well be a symptom of general management disorganization or may simply be the result of poor planning on the part of one individual. It is your responsibility as a potential employee to be aware of these signals and make your decisions accordingly.

If you find that the interviewer is reading from your résumé rather than discussing the job with you, you can guide the interviewer back to a dialogue. Simply say something like, "Ms. Jones, I would like to tell you about some relevant experience I gained during my recent internship. It applies to the kind of experience you are seeking in a candidate." This will help create a dialogue and will give you an opportunity to talk about your strengths and experiences and how you can add value to the team you hope to join.

By all means, bring at least one copy of your résumé to the interview. Occasionally, at the close of an interview, an interviewer will express an interest in circulating a résumé to several departments, and you could then offer the copy you brought. Sometimes, an interview appointment provides an opportunity to meet others in the organization who may express an interest in you and your background, and it may be helpful to follow up with a copy of your résumé. Our best advice, however, is to keep it out of sight until needed or requested.

Employer Information

Whether your interview is for graduate school admission, an overseas corporate position, or a position with a local company, it is important to know something about the employer or the organization. Keeping in mind that the interview is relatively brief and that you will hopefully have other interviews with other organizations, it is important to keep your research in proportion. If secondary interviews are called for, you will have additional time to do further research. For the first interview, it is helpful to know the organization's mission, goals, size, scope of operations, and so forth. Your research may uncover recent areas of challenge or particular successes that may help to fuel the interview. Use the "What Do They Call the Job You Want?" section of Chapter 3, your library, and your career or guidance office to help you locate this information in the most efficient way possible. Don't be shy in asking advice of these counseling and guidance professionals on how best to spend your preparation time. With some practice, you'll soon learn how much information is enough and which kinds of information are most useful to you.

Interview Content

We've already discussed how it can help to think of the interview as an important conversation—one that, as with any conversation, you want to find pleasant and interesting and to leave you with a good feeling. But because this conversation is especially important, the information that's exchanged is critical to its success. What do you want them to know about you? What do you need to know about them? What interview technique do you need to particularly pay attention to? How do you want to manage the close of the interview? What steps will follow in the hiring process?

Except for the professional interviewer, most of us find interviewing stressful and anxiety-provoking. Developing a strategy before you begin interviewing will help you relieve some stress and anxiety. One particular strategy that has worked for many and may work for you is interviewing by objective. Before you interview, write down three to five goals you would like to achieve for that interview. They may be technique goals: smile a little more, have a firmer handshake, be sure to ask about the next stage in the interview process before leaving. They may be content-oriented goals: find out about the company's current challenges and opportunities; be sure to speak of your recent research, writing experiences, or foreign travel. Whatever your goals, jot down a few of them as goals for each interview.

Most people find that in trying to achieve these few goals, their interviewing technique becomes more organized and focused. After the interview, the most common question friends and family ask is "How did it go?" With this technique, you have an indication of whether you met *your* goals for the meeting, not just some vague idea of how it went. Chances are, if you accomplished what you wanted to, it improved the quality of the entire interview. As you continue to interview, you will want to revise your goals to continue improving your interview skills.

Now, add to the concept of the significant conversation the idea of a beginning, a middle, and a closing and you will have two thoughts that will give your interview a distinctive character. Be sure to make your introduction warm and cordial. Say your full name (and if it's a difficult-to-pronounce name, help the interviewer to pronounce it) and make certain you know your interviewer's name and how to pronounce it. Most interviews begin with some "soft talk" about the weather, chat about the candidate's trip to the interview site, or national events. This is done as a courtesy to relax both you and the interviewer, to get you talking, and to generally try to defuse the atmosphere of excessive tension. Try to be yourself, engage in the conversation, and don't try to second-guess the interviewer. This is simply what it appears to be—casual conversation.

Once you and the interviewer move on to exchange more serious information in the middle part of the interview, the two most important concerns become your ability to handle challenging questions and your success at asking meaningful ones. Interviewer questions will probably fall into one of three categories: personal assessment and career direction, academic assessment, and knowledge of the employer. Here are a few examples of questions in each category:

Personal Assessment and Career Direction
1. What motivates you to put forth your best effort?
2. What do you consider to be your greatest strengths and weaknesses?
3. What qualifications do you have that make you think you will be successful in this career?

Academic Assessment
1. What led you to choose your major?
2. What subjects did you like best and least? Why?
3. How has your college experience prepared you for this career?

Knowledge of the Employer
1. What do you think it takes to be successful in an organization like ours?
2. In what ways do you think you can make a contribution to our organization?
3. Why did you choose to seek a position with this organization?

The interviewer wants a response to each question but is also gauging your enthusiasm, preparedness, and willingness to communicate. In each response you should provide some information about yourself that can be related to the employer's needs. A common mistake is to give too much information. Answer each question completely, but be careful not to run on too long with extensive details or examples.

Questions About Underdeveloped Skills

Most employers interview people who have met some minimum criteria of education and experience. They interview candidates to see who they are, to learn what kind of personality they exhibit, and to get some sense of how they might fit into the existing organization. It may be that you are asked about skills the employer hopes to find and that you have not documented. Maybe it's grant-writing experience, knowledge of the European political system, or a knowledge of the film world.

To questions about skills and experiences you don't have, answer honestly and forthrightly and try to offer some additional information about skills you do have. For example, perhaps the employer is disappointed you have no grant-writing experience. An honest answer may be as follows:

No, unfortunately, I was never in a position to acquire those skills. I do understand something of the complexities of the grant-writing process and feel confident that my attention to detail, careful reading skills, and strong writing would make grants a wonderful challenge in a new job. I think I could get up on the learning curve quickly.

The employer hears an honest admission of lack of experience but is reassured by some specific skill details that do relate to grant writing and a confident manner that suggests enthusiasm and interest in a challenge.

For many students, questions about their possible contribution to an employer's organization can prove challenging. Because your education has probably not included specific training for a job, you need to review your academic record and select capabilities you have developed in your major that an employer can appreciate. For example, perhaps you read well and can analyze and condense what you've read into smaller, more focused pieces. That could be valuable. Or maybe you did some serious research and you know you have valuable investigative skills. Your public speaking might be highly developed and you might use visual aids appropriately and effectively. Or maybe your skill at correspondence, memos, and messages is effective. Whatever it is, you must take it out of the academic context and put it into a new, employer-friendly context so your interviewer can best judge how you could help the organization.

Exhibiting knowledge of the organization will, without a doubt, show the interviewer that you are interested enough in the available position to have done some legwork in preparation for the interview. Remember, it is not necessary to know every detail of the organization's history but rather to have a general knowledge about why it is in business and how the industry is faring.

Sometime during the interview, generally after the midway point, you'll be asked if you have any questions for the interviewer. Your questions will tell the employer much about your attitude and your desire to understand the organization's expectations so you can compare them to your own strengths. The following are just a few questions you might want to ask:

1. What is the communication style of the organization? (meetings, memos, and so forth)
2. What would a typical day in this position be like for me?
3. What have been some of the interesting challenges and opportunities your organization has recently faced?

Most interviews draw to a natural closing point, so be careful not to prolong the discussion. At a signal from the interviewer, wind up your presentation, express your appreciation for the opportunity, and be sure to ask what the next stage in the process will be. When can you expect to hear from them? Will they be conducting second-tier interviews? If you are interested and haven't heard, would they mind a phone call? Be sure to collect a business card with the name and phone number of your interviewer. On your way out, you might have an opportunity to pick up organizational literature you haven't seen before.

With the right preparation—a thorough self-assessment, professional clothing, and employer information—you'll be able to set and achieve the goals you have established for the interview process.

Interview Follow-Up

Quite often there is a considerable time lag between interviewing for a position and being hired or, in the case of the networker, between your phone call or letter to a possible contact and the opportunity of a meeting. This can be frustrating. "Why aren't they contacting me?" "I thought I'd get another interview, but no one has telephoned." "Am I out of the running?" You don't know what is happening.

Consider the Differing Perspectives

Of course, there is another perspective—that of the networker or hiring organization. Organizations are complex, with multiple tasks that need to be accomplished each day. Hiring is a discrete activity that does not occur as frequently as other job assignments. The hiring process might have to take second place to other, more immediate organizational needs. Although it may be very important to you, and it is certainly ultimately significant to the employer, other issues such as fiscal management, planning and product development, employer vacation periods, or financial constraints may prevent an organization or individual within that organization from acting on your employment or your request for information as quickly as you or they would prefer.

Use Your Communication Skills

Good communication is essential here to resolve any anxieties, and the responsibility is on you, the job or information seeker. Too many job seekers and networkers offer as an excuse that they don't want to "bother" the organization by writing letters or calling. Let us assure you here and now, once and for all, that if you are troubling an organization by over-communicating, someone will indicate that situation to you quite clearly. If not, you can only assume you are a worthwhile prospect and the employer appreciates being reminded of your availability and interest. Let's look at follow-up practices in the job interview process and the networking situation separately.

Following Up on the Employment Interview

A brief thank-you note following an interview is an excellent and polite way to begin a series of follow-up communications with a potential employer with whom you have interviewed and want to remain in touch. It should be just that—a thank-you for a good meeting. If you failed to mention some fact or experience during your interview that you think might add to your candidacy, you may use this note to do that. However, this should be essentially a note whose overall tone is appreciative and, if appropriate, indicative of a continuing interest in pursuing any opportunity that may exist with that organization. It is one of the few pieces of business correspondence that may be handwritten, but always use plain, good-quality, standard-size paper.

If, however, at this point you are no longer interested in the employer, the thank-you note is an appropriate time to indicate that. You are under no obligation to identify any reason for not continuing to pursue employment with that organization, but if you are so inclined to indicate your professional reasons (pursuing other employers more akin to your interests, looking for greater income production than this employer can provide, a different geographic location), you certainly may. It should not be written with an eye to negotiation, for it will not be interpreted as such.

As part of your interview closing, you should have taken the initiative to establish lines of communication for continuing information about your candidacy. If you asked permission to telephone, wait a week following your thank-you note, then telephone your contact simply to inquire how things are progressing on your employment status. The feedback you receive here should be taken at face value. If your interviewer simply has no information, he or she will tell you so and indicate whether you should call again and when. Don't be discouraged if this should continue over some period of time.

If during this time something occurs that you think improves or changes your candidacy (some new qualification or experience you may have had), including any offers from other organizations, by all means telephone or write to inform the employer about this. In the case of an offer from a competing but less desirable or equally desirable organization, telephone your contact, explain what has happened, express your real interest in the organization, and inquire whether some determination on your employment might be made before you must respond to this other offer. An organization that is truly interested in you may be moved to make a decision about your candidacy. Equally possible is the scenario in which they are not yet ready to make a decision and so advise you to take the offer that has been presented. Again, you have no ethical alternative but to deal with the information presented in a straightforward manner.

When accepting other employment, be sure to contact any employers still actively considering you and inform them of your new job. Thank them graciously for their consideration. There are many other job seekers out there just like you who will benefit from having their candidacy improved when others bow out of the race. Who knows, you might at some future time have occasion to interact professionally with one of the organizations with which you sought employment. How embarrassing it would be to have someone remember you as the candidate who failed to notify them that you were taking a job elsewhere!

In all of your follow-up communications, keep good notes of whom you spoke with, when you called, and any instructions that were given about return communications. This will prevent any misunderstandings and provide you with good records of what has transpired.

Job Offer Considerations

For many recent college graduates, the thrill of their first job and, for some, the most substantial regular income they have ever earned seems an excess of good fortune coming at once. To question that first income or to be critical in any way of the conditions of employment at the time of the initial offer seems like looking a gift horse in the mouth. It doesn't seem to occur to many new hires even to attempt to negotiate any aspect of their first job. And, as many employers who deal with entry-level jobs for recent college graduates will readily confirm, the reality is that there simply isn't much movement in salary available to these new college recruits. The entry-level hire generally does not have an employment track record on a professional level to provide any leverage for negotiation. Real negotiations on salary, benefits, retirement provisions, and so forth come to those with significant employment records at higher income levels.

Of course, the job offer is more than just money. It can be composed of geographic assignment, duties and responsibilities, training, benefits, health and medical insurance, educational assistance, car allowance or company vehicle, and a host of other items. All of this is generally detailed in the formal letter that presents the final job offer. In most cases this is a follow-up to a personal phone call from the employer representative who has been principally responsible for your hiring process.

That initial telephone offer is certainly binding as a verbal agreement, but most firms follow up with a detailed letter outlining the most significant parts of your employment contract. You may, of course, choose to respond immediately at the time of the telephone offer (which would be considered a binding oral contract), but you will also be required to formally answer the letter of offer with a letter of acceptance, restating the salient elements of the employer's description of your position, salary, and benefits. This ensures that both parties are clear on the terms and conditions of employment and remuneration and any other outstanding aspects of the job offer.

Is This the Job You Want?
Most new employees will respond affirmatively in writing, glad to be in the position to accept employment. If you've worked hard to get the offer and the job market is tight, other offers may not be in sight, so you will say, "Yes,

I accept!" What is important here is that the job offer you accept be one that does fit your particular needs, values, and interests as you've outlined them in your self-assessment process. Moreover, it should be a job that will not only use your skills and education but also challenge you to develop new skills and talents.

Jobs are sometimes accepted too hastily, for the wrong reasons, and without proper scrutiny by the applicant. For example, an individual might readily accept a sales job only to find the continual rejection by potential clients unendurable. An office worker might realize within weeks the constraints of a desk job and yearn for more activity. Employment is an important part of our lives. It is, for most of our adult lives, our most continuous productive activity. We want to make good choices based on the right criteria.

If you have a low tolerance for risk, a job based on commission will certainly be very anxiety-provoking. If being near your family is important, issues of relocation could present a decision crisis for you. If you're an adventurous person, a job with frequent travel would provide needed excitement and be very desirable. The importance of income, the need to continue your education, your personal health situation—all of these have an impact on whether the job you are considering will ultimately meet your needs. Unless you've spent some time understanding and thinking about these issues, it will be difficult to evaluate offers you do receive.

More important, if you make a decision that you cannot tolerate and feel you must leave that job, you will then have both unemployment and self-esteem issues to contend with. These will combine to make the next job search tough going, indeed. So make your acceptance a carefully considered decision.

Negotiate Your Offer

It may be that there is some aspect of your job offer that is not particularly attractive to you. Perhaps there is no relocation allotment to help you move your possessions, and this presents some financial hardship for you. It may be that the health insurance is less than you had hoped. Your initial assignment may be different from what you expected, either in its location or in the duties and responsibilities that comprise it. Or it may simply be that the salary is less than you anticipated. Other considerations may be your official starting date of employment, vacation time, evening hours, dates of training programs or schools, and other concerns.

If you are considering not accepting the job because of some item or items in the job offer "package" that do not meet your needs, you should know that most employers emphatically wish that you would bring that issue to their attention. It may be that the employer can alter it to make the offer more agreeable for you. In some cases it cannot be changed. In any event the employer would generally like to have the opportunity to try to remedy a difficulty rather than risk losing a good potential employee over an issue that might have been resolved. After all, they have spent time and funds in securing your services, and they certainly deserve an opportunity to resolve any possible differences.

Honesty is the best approach in discussing any objections or uneasiness you might have over the employer's offer. Having received your formal offer in writing, contact your employer representative and indicate your particular dissatisfaction in a straightforward manner. For example, you might explain that while you are very interested in being employed by this organization, the salary (or any other benefit) is less than you have determined you require. State the terms you need, and listen to the response. You may be asked to put this in writing, or you may be asked to hold off until the firm can decide on a response. If you are dealing with a senior representative of the organization, one who has been involved in hiring for some time, you may get an immediate response or a solid indication of possible outcomes.

Perhaps the issue is one of relocation. Your initial assignment is in the Midwest, and because you had indicated a strong West Coast preference, you are surprised at the actual assignment. You might simply indicate that while you understand the need for the company to assign you based on its needs, you are disappointed and had hoped to be placed on the West Coast. You could inquire if that were still possible and, if not, would it be reasonable to expect a West Coast relocation in the future.

If your request is presented in a reasonable way, most employers will not see this as jeopardizing your offer. If they can agree to your proposal, they will. If not, they will simply tell you so, and you may choose to continue your candidacy with them or remove yourself from consideration. The choice will be up to you.

Some firms will adjust benefits within their parameters to meet the candidate's need if at all possible. If a candidate requires a relocation cost allowance, he or she may be asked to forgo tuition benefits for the first year to accomplish this adjustment. An increase in life insurance may be adjusted by some other benefit trade-off; perhaps a family dental plan is not needed. In these decisions you are called upon, sometimes under time pressure, to know how you value these issues and how important each is to you.

Many employers find they are more comfortable negotiating for candidates who have unique qualifications or who bring especially needed expertise to the organization. Employers hiring large numbers of entry-level college graduates may be far more reluctant to accommodate any changes in offer conditions. They are well supplied with candidates with similar education and experience so that if rejected by one candidate, they can draw new candidates from an ample labor pool.

Compare Offers

The condition of the economy, the job seeker's academic major and particular geographic job market, and individual needs and demands for certain employment conditions may not provide more than one job offer at a time. Some job seekers may feel that no reasonable offer should go unaccepted for the simple fear there won't be another.

In a tough job market, or if the job you seek is not widely available, or when your job search goes on too long and becomes difficult to sustain financially and emotionally, it may be necessary to accept an inferior offer. The alternative is continued unemployment. Even here, when you feel you don't have a choice, you can at least understand that in accepting this particular offer, there may be limitations and conditions you don't appreciate. At the time of acceptance, there were no other alternatives, but you can begin to use that position to gain the experience and talent to move toward a more attractive position.

Sometimes, however, more than one offer is received, and the candidate has the luxury of choice. If the job seeker knows what he or she wants and has done the necessary self-assessment honestly and thoroughly, it may be clear that one of the offers conforms more closely to those expressed wants and needs.

However, if, as so often happens, the offers are similar in terms of conditions and salary, the question then becomes which organization might provide the necessary climate, opportunities, and advantages for your professional development and growth. This is the time when solid employer research and astute questioning during the interviews really pay off. How much did you learn about the employer through your own research and skillful questioning? When the interviewer asked during the interview "Do you have any questions?" did you ask the kinds of questions that would help resolve a choice between one organization and another? Just as an employer must decide among numerous applicants, so must the applicant learn to assess the potential employer. Both are partners in the job search.

Reneging on an Offer

An especially disturbing occurrence for employers and career counseling professionals is when a job seeker formally (either orally or by written contract) accepts employment with one organization and later reneges on the agreement and goes with another employer.

There are all kinds of rationalizations offered for this unethical behavior. None of them satisfies. The sad irony is that what the job seeker is willing to do to the employer—make a promise and then break it—he or she would be outraged to have done to him- or herself: have the job offer pulled. It is a very bad way to begin a career. It suggests the individual has not taken the time to do the necessary self-assessment and self-awareness exercises to think and judge critically. The new offer taken may, in fact, be no better or worse than the one refused. You should be aware that there have been incidents of legal action following job candidates' reneging on an offer. This adds a very sour note to what should be a harmonious beginning of a lifelong adventure.

PART TWO

THE CAREER PATHS

Introduction to the English Career Paths

There is perhaps no major less subject to academic fads and fancies than English. It has always been not only a mainstay of the college curriculum, but also the foundation of work in many other academic areas. Of all the liberal arts degrees, it opens the most doors and makes the graduate versatile and highly employable in any number of entry-level positions. The importance of English skills in all academic disciplines has been heightened by initiatives such as writing across the curriculum and other similar programs designed to emphasize to faculty in all subject areas the importance of writing skills and the need to introduce writing exercises into all fields of study.

Applying Your Skills to the World of Work

Spoken and written English are important in every aspect of employment for every level of worker. Conferences, one-on-one meetings, memoranda, short and long reports, agenda, instructions, training materials, and a host of other communications mark every decision in the workplace. Video productions; user's manuals; procedures, specifications, and similar technical materials; and promotional materials all benefit from the attention of someone who is proficient in English usage. Business and industry leaders consistently call for applicants with a solid command of written and spoken English. It is what they need most and what they see least in interviewing sessions.

Forty years ago, an English degree from a four-year school was all a graduate needed to launch a successful career. The vanguard of that generation are now at the senior levels of their careers and are anticipating retirement.

A review of the biographies of many leaders and innovators from past generations across a number of occupational areas shows this to be true. What is equally true is that the English graduate today, armed with an aggressive and disciplined approach to the job search, can find an equally wide array of employment opportunities as the graduate of forty years ago.

English is full of possibilities for a career based on solid skill with the written and spoken word. English can be marketing when expressed through the medium of copywriting. English can be computer science through technical writing. English can be newspaper reporting or book publishing through the techniques of editing and proofreading. English can be historical through the interpretation and archiving of ancient English and near-English texts. English can be international commerce as well, because English is increasingly the language of global business. English can be art through creative writing in fiction, poetry, and prose. What other degree offers so much?

Although today's English graduates do well in their chosen careers, as has been frequently documented, these new graduates have also been found to have difficulties in making the transition from college to the workplace. The root of this problem may be confusion over what has been learned in college and its transferability to the workplace. English as a major is not job training; it is an education in the history and grandeur of the English language and what has been created from it. The content of this academic major, in and of itself, is only immediately transferable to occupations such as editing, writing, publishing, and teaching English.

Let's look again at your English education to see what is there for the employer. Of course, you have developed writing skills; these are very important to any employer. Look deeper. Behind writing is skill in research—understanding how to use informational resources and seek out the data you need. This investigative skill is an important function in all employment and is equally valuable. You also learned critical thinking: you needed to decide what pieces of information to include and not to include in your writing to have the most impact. Style, too, became a consideration as you learned to present your written material from a particular point of view. Style causes the reader to retain the importance of the writing and to return to it again and again.

Reading, too, loomed large in the educational process for an English major. But how can that reading help in the employment picture? There is reading for pleasure and reading for content. Each morning, the president of the United States reads a digest of important news culled for him from many, many sources. These original sources were read by others who selected critical pieces for the president to read. Or, after reading, they were edited down to more concise expressions of the original for speed and convenience. All of this is within the capabilities of the English major. The president isn't the only one who needs to have material read, selected, and digested.

But there is, of course, more to reading than this. English majors develop an appreciation of literary styles throughout history—the Old English of Beowulf, the Middle English of Chaucer, or the contemporary prose of Joyce Carol Oates. The sweep of human history has been conveyed in both fiction and nonfiction, and the English major whose own vocabulary has been enriched through that study can use that vocabulary in the workplace.

Freewriting, keeping a journal, college newspaper work, or a writing internship can all contribute to the finely honed communication skills that allow you to say what you want, directly, clearly, and concisely. Every employer needs those abilities in its workers. But be ready to express these wonderful skills in a context the employer understands and finds desirable. To talk about your research skills in the context of the tradition of romance novelists would not make much sense to a newspaper editor. For example, research that an editor could appreciate would be background work for an article on AIDS. Perhaps you have researched the lineage of published books, films, and short stories that used AIDS as a metaphor for loss. Describing this research to a potential employer in the newspaper industry would be very meaningful.

You will need to isolate each of your skills and find a new context in which to explain their importance. That context may be in one of the career paths outlined here:

1. Writing, editing, and publishing
2. Teaching
3. Advertising and public relations
4. Business administration and management
5. Technical writing

Or it might be something entirely different, like screenwriting. Whatever you choose, you will learn how to make a case for your English degree.

A Special Note: Computers and the English Major

A crucial skill set needed in all of the career paths presented in this book is education and training in the use of computer technology. More than simply a new technique for inscribing the English language, computer technology is determining language forms itself. Whether it is e-books that can be read online or downloaded to a variety of devices; business intelligence software and solutions including enterprise reporting, query and analysis, data integration, and performance management tools; or new software that can help antiterrorism planners determine how best to allocate limited resources, English majors at a minimum need to possess a solid understanding of word-processing, spreadsheet, and database software. Employers will want to know that you are comfortable with computer technology and willing to learn industry-specific technology. Throughout the following discussion of career paths, we cite many advertisements for jobs that seek English graduates but also demand a high level of computer facility.

Computers are omnipresent in the world of professional writers. Fiction and nonfiction writers, poets, and word artists of all kinds use this technology. Specialized research studies in graduate school areas such as comparative literature have been greatly enhanced by computer search skills.

Research, a staple of the undergraduate and graduate-level English student's academic program, is now commonly done electronically via the Internet and CD-ROM technology, which are increasingly taking the place of printed reference materials because of durability, ease in cataloging, and cost.

The message here is crystal clear. If you are still in school as you read this, any computer skills you can acquire will be to your distinct advantage in the job search process. If you have already graduated, do what you can through community programs, self-study, and continuing education to learn some of the software packages you'll see mentioned in this book. If you are employed, take advantage of professional development opportunities and your educational benefits and learn all you can about the technology that's available. It's a natural and essential adjunct to your English degree.

Path I:
Writing, Editing,
and Publishing

As an English major, creativity and visualization should come relatively easily to you. So let's do an exercise using both of these skills. Place yourself in the middle of Times Square in New York City. Look around you. What do you see? Listen to the people going by—what do you hear? Then, on the Ginza in Tokyo, the Place de la Concorde in Paris, or the Spanish Steps in Rome, along with the other visual and auditory reminders of a shrinking world, you will see and hear English in constant use. English is preeminent in the United States, Great Britain, and Australia and is increasingly dominant around the world as the language of technology, business, and industry.

Let's return to Times Square. We go into a major bookstore and immediately are impressed with the breadth and scope of publications available: books, manuals, newspapers, and magazines all written, edited, and published using English skills. But even the largest general bookstore contains only the tip of the iceberg of published materials. Much more is published in the fields of education and industry, which rival the consumer sector for employment possibilities. We are an information society, and much of that information is written.

We step into a corporate office tower, and at the reception desk we find the corporation newspaper or journal, an in-house publication written, edited, and produced for its employees. Many mid- to large-sized organizations need a number of in-house communication organs to share information about standards, employees and their activities (both professional and personal), new developments, and prospects for growth. These publications serve as vital communications links in large organizations and also help to build the esprit de corps essential to an organization's success. The professionalism of these corporate publications, the technical resources available to produce them, and the corporate time and attention lavished on them rival the commercial publishing industry in quality.

We find ourselves outside the showroom of a major computer retailer. The Internet today holds perhaps more writing, editing, and publishing opportunities than all other fields combined. There are countless Web magazines, journals, articles, and texts produced by people like you. And if you're thinking that working in the computer industry means you'll need superior computer skills, you're mostly correct! Not only does working in this industry require superb computer skills, but it'll keep you on the cutting edge for the future. Many of these "cyber employers" are going to expect you to apply for your job on the Web, e-mail your résumé to them, and have a professional home page of your own that they can visit to learn more about you. So get ready.

Next door at a major music and video retailer, we find on the counter a free magazine filled with articles, interviews, and behind-the-scenes views of the music industry. Designed to excite customers about the products and services of these retailers, it is, nevertheless, a substantial piece of publishing with all the editorial content, graphics, and readability of a weekly newsmagazine. The magazine is published only after careful story planning, assignment of writers, research checks for accuracy and legality, and the solicitation of advertising sponsors. Working on such a publication would be an excellent training ground for anyone contemplating a move to *Newsweek*, *Time*, or any other well-known magazine venture.

Continuing down the street, we stop in front of a large appliance store and watch on a bank of TVs the many duplications of a network news reader's countenance as he or she reports the day's events. We should remember the support staff working behind the scenes at such a news-gathering organization: reading and selecting pieces from the news wires, editing the field reports of stringers and reporters, and putting together written texts, all under intense time pressure. We discover here in broadcast news an entirely different industry hiring employees interested in careers in writing, editing, and publishing.

The television picture blinks, and the scene changes. A reporter is now interviewing a newly published author, and we realize once again that working within an organization is not your only career option. You might have your own story to tell from either facts or fantasy. The world of freelance writing is alive and well, and although only the strong survive the entrepreneurial demands of freelancing, those who do, do so very well. Many pursue freelance writing on their own while regularly employed in the hopes that a publication will launch them into a career of pure writing; however, some find it difficult to balance writing with a regular job.

We hear a barker farther down the street and turn to see someone working at a kiosk filled with newspapers, magazines, and journals. We think of all the writers, editors, and publishers who have come together to produce all this material who depend on the same set of writing, critical thinking, and creative skills we polished as English majors. As we look over the selection of materials, we see some of these newspapers and magazines are in English but are published overseas. The *Japan Times* and the journal *Kyoto* are among these publications, and we realize that publishing in English is not something done only in the United States.

Definition of the Career Path

Our walk around Times Square has opened up unlimited prospects for us to consider in the fields of writing, editing, and publishing. Each of these arenas—newspapers and magazines, arts and entertainment, book publishing, freelance writing, and radio and television—offers employment prospects. Within these varied employment fields are countless employers of all sizes with staffs numbering from two or three to thousands. The size and scope of the employer will have much to do with the range of skills you are able to employ in your particular job and will, in turn, affect how you are judged as a job candidate.

For example, let's examine television and radio. In a small station, you may find yourself writing copy for the announcers, researching and editing copy, helping an advertiser write an effective commercial, editing news stories as they come off the wire, and writing intros and segues for different parts of the broadcast. In a larger organization, your first job may simply be checking copy for accuracy or legal implications. Although your salary and benefits might be better in a large organization than if you worked in a small station, and perhaps your advancement possibilities are equally excellent, your initial assignments may be very limited in scope.

Regardless of the size of the organization, it is a safe bet that one skill set you will be called on to use will be computer skills. A glance at the following job listings graphically shows the omnipresence of employers' demands that anyone working with English skills and written communication be computer literate. The software may be different from what you've known, but the elements are the same, and the employer will expect you to be conversant with word-processing and perhaps desktop publishing capabilities. If you're still in school and have neglected these particular skills, take advantage of your remaining time and acquire the necessary familiarity to meet most computer requirements. Some requirements we pulled from recent job listings are shown below:

- Requires keyboarding skills
- Must be capable of working in a Windows environment
- Knowledge of basic HTML and ability to code by hand are required
- Proficiency with Microsoft Word and the Internet for research and fact-checking required
- Must have strong knowledge and use of Macintosh MS Office (Word, Excel, Entourage)
- Must have aptitude for learning new software programs

Even though all the career paths we will discuss in this section rely heavily on English skills, they don't all focus on the same skills, nor do they value the same areas of expertise within the general area of English. Some place emphasis on the technical aspects of writing English: syntax, subject and tense agreement, point of view, vocabulary, spelling, and the parts of speech and their correct use in writing. Others are less concerned with technical details and more focused on style, imagery, metaphor, and other aspects of writing that can further the tone of a piece, keep the writing true to itself, and accomplish the author's intention. Others emphasize critical skills in reducing or expanding a piece of writing to fit an external demand of time or space. They require the ability to condense or extend the author's message without compromising the integrity of the piece. Still others focus on the facts and details of what has been written. Is it accurate? Did it happen just that way? Were those people all there? Did he or she actually say just that? Has it been reported anywhere else? Can we say this? Attention must be paid to countless other details about a piece of writing to prevent a later controversy or contradiction that might take the focus away from the author's overall message.

Still others are concerned with the challenging task of taking densely written material or complicated prose and making it clear to the average reader. And others look at a piece of writing to help in selecting art, illustrations, book cover designs, and typefaces that are most suited to the author's intention and style.

Now take all these different realizations of editing, writing, and publishing and multiply them by the various industries in which they can occur:

news organizations, broadcasting, the entertainment industry, theater, text-book and trade book publishing, corporate in-house communications, and so on, and you begin to understand the number of possibilities.

The field of writing, editing, and publishing jobs is vast, and although five different career professionals might all share an English degree in common, it's a safe bet they are all using their education in a different way and emphasizing different facets of their academic preparation as they go about their jobs. To illustrate the possibilities in the areas of writing, editing, and publishing, we will examine four possible career paths that are representative of the myriad possibilities for English majors.

To get a better idea of what it is like to work in the areas that interest you, use your alumni association or career office to create a network of graduates in these fields. Ask if you can visit alumni at their place of work or even spend a day "shadowing" them as they go about their jobs. Pay attention to the pace of their day, the nature of their duties and assignments, and the work climate. Try the job on. Then go back and do your research about who hires people to do these jobs, how much they pay, and what the outlook for employment will be.

Add to this your own values and interests, your objective evaluation of your past experiences, and your skills in your academic major, and you will have developed a solid base from which to begin your exploration and eventual entry into one of these fields. Your commitment to one over another is not a matter of great risk, however. Whereas in medicine it's rather difficult for an orthopedic surgeon to easily change to internal medicine, that is not the case in the fields of editing, publishing, and writing. There are many crossover skills and many correspondences and overlaps within individual jobs. Your experience in a different field may, in fact, enhance your desirability to a new employer as you'll bring fresh perspective, insight, and critical judgment to your job while still using many of the same techniques and skills you have in your previous work.

Reporting

This job attracts many applicants because the reporter's job is challenging, ever-changing, and fast-paced and keeps you always ahead of the general public in knowing what's going on. Reporters must feel a deep commitment to communicating news and informing people of the state of the world. Though there is desk work, it would be erroneous to assume that reporting is a "desk job." Reporters may work in either corporate communications or more traditional news organizations. Consider the following job advertisements found recently on the Internet at sites such as journalismjobs.com:

Reporter to Cover Courts. Growing legal news service is looking for a reporter to cover state and federal courts in and around Salt Lake City. Legal background not required, but demonstrated interest and ability in writing necessary. Job entails going to state and federal courts in downtown area every afternoon, as well as driving to courts in surrounding counties. To apply, e-mail a cover letter, résumé, and two nonfiction writing samples, attached in Word format.

Education Reporter. Do you want to become a subject-matter expert who digs deep into stories to provide specialized information to niche audiences? One of the country's fastest growing multimedia companies needs education reporters to gather, analyze, and synthesize information for advice-driven, subscription-based publications. Enjoy significant autonomy covering complex issues in a deadline-driven but collaborative atmosphere. We have a casual workplace and excellent benefits. Fax your résumé.

Business Reporter. Looking for an energetic, hardworking business reporter who will excel in covering a variety of business beats, personalities, and trends for our 115,000 daily/145,000 Sunday paper. Successful candidate will write breaking news stories and business features for daily business sections and specialized weekly sections. Looking for a thorough and accurate reporter and a clear, concise, and engaging writer who communicates honestly and constructively with the public and staff. Send résumé, cover letter, five clips, and three references by e-mail.

Reporter. Respected regional agricultural magazine seeks energetic reporter to cover agriculture. Must be a strong writer and adept at managing time and multiple assignments. Must have genuine interest in agriculture and general knowledge of trends in the industry. Photography and online skills desirable. Requires some travel. Send writing samples and résumé.

Working Conditions. Most reporting, whether in a corporate or news organization setting, is done under deadlines of time and of space. Consequently, there is usually a high degree of stress in fulfilling these outwardly imposed constraints. When several reporters are working together, each on his or her own schedule, this sense of anxiety, noise, and general confusion is apt to multiply. Additionally, one seldom has the luxury of working on one article, story, or project at a time. More likely, you will be juggling several different assignments, all at varying stages. One may be in fact-checking and another may simply be a story outline. When one requires research, another needs a human touch. Reporting involves myriad assignments and myriad deadlines, all subject to change and acceleration or postponement. Significant telephone work and much time on the road characterize a reporter's working day.

Training and Qualifications. Certainly, writing skills and the ability to work under pressure are paramount in most hiring officials' minds when looking for a promising reporter. But others may look for many other indications of possible success in this line of work: intelligence, quickness, desire to succeed, and dedication. Aggressiveness and willingness to ask the difficult questions are important, too. Reporters often don't get an opportunity to revisit a situation, so the correct information must be gathered in one meeting. That takes thinking ahead, planning, and thoroughness.

Earnings. In a corporate setting, reporters are often found in the public relations department. MediaBistro.com (mediabistro.com) reports by region entry-level salaries for small to midsized firms having PR departments: Northeast: $35,000; South: $33,000; Midwest: $36,000; and West: $36,000. Many reporters working for news organizations belong to the Newspaper Guild, an arm of the AFL-CIO. The Guild reports, on its website (newsguild.org), top minimum salary information for reporters who have a given number of years of experience. Starting minimum weekly pay ranged from $387.50 at the Utica, New York, *Observer-Dispatch* to $1,264 at the *Times Colonist* in Victoria, British Columbia.

Editing

Decisions, decisions, and more decisions characterize the editorial role. Making decisions, being comfortable with them, and sticking to them are important to an editor's success. Editors decide what stays and what goes, what's important and what's not. In newspaper work, many editors come up from the reporting ranks, whereas in publishing, editors are often groomed to work with one particular type of material or a unique cluster of authors. Editors provide guidance, in the newsroom or in consultation with a reporter, and their job is to oversee the operation and birth of a printed product and to understand what is appropriate for publication and what is not. Assistant and associate editors also double-check facts and statistics used in the text for accuracy. Position titles include editorial assistant, assistant editor, associate editor, editor, copyeditor, and senior editor.

Assistant Editor. World's leading electronic distributor of full-text news releases seeks assistant editor for [large metro area] bureau. Edit, process, format, and proofread clients' news releases. Handle phone duty and troubleshoot customer issues. Requires excellent skills in customer service, proofreading, communications, and keyboarding. Bachelor's degree required. Must possess ability to handle multiple tasks in fast-paced, deadline driven environment; must excel under pressure.

Editorial Assistant. Custom magazines and association membership directories. Work with managing editor to develop and help manage all content for client magazines and directories. Will be involved in entire process to ensure quality standards, deadlines, and client objectives are met. Also responsible for writing content and editing content written by others.

Assistant Editor. Business-to-business travel-oriented information publisher. Input and edit information submitted by worldwide correspondents. Research and fact-check using Internet. Knowledge of AP style and travel experience a plus. Requires strong written communications skills, good command of consistent style, and ability to produce appropriate and grammatically correct copy.

Working Conditions. Editing is a focused occupation in which distractions must be avoided. To edit well is to take on the writer's persona, to carefully concentrate on the intention of the work, and to make what changes might be necessary in a seamless, unobtrusive manner. To edit well is to be anonymous. Although you may have seen editors effusively thanked by their authors in interviews and in book dedications, it is difficult for readers of the finished work to know what transformations the editor is responsible for when they read the final product.

Training and Qualifications. The ability to see the overall picture, be it a novel, short story, or newspaper edition, and the ability to make quick decisions about choice, tone, quality, and inclusion or exclusion of detail are important in editorial work. Very often, the editor represents the publisher and must balance his or her artistic judgment against institutional goals and considerations. The newspaper editor assigns work and maintains a flowchart of story assignments and completion dates. The book editor works closely with the author and will be involved in every aspect of publication, including technical printing details. Superior communications skills, both verbal and written, strong interpersonal skills, experience, and judgment are the hallmarks of the discerning editor.

Earnings. Any salary wizard or salary calculator can provide current salary information for the various editing job titles in specific geographic areas. Given a recent degree and limited work experience, the salary to use is the number given by the calculator for the 25th percentile. The American Society of Business Publications Editors' salary survey currently shows junior-level editorial positions starting at $30,300. *Publisher's Weekly* (publishers weekly.com) publishes an annual salary survey that reports the average salary for a variety of positions. Be sure to check the latest survey available.

Researching

Many different kinds of research work, including historical research, literary research, and scientific research, integrate training in English/writing and the critical judgment and investigative skills developed through analytical and research paper writing in college. Research provides the framework for much prose production and is often essential in the outline of a particular project. Most writing, including fiction, requires research support.

Open a copy of any popular weekly newsmagazine or daily paper and scan the stories of interest. Now read them more carefully. Note how many refer to statistics, events, dates, and all kinds of facts that had to be verified and documented by someone. Sometimes this research is done simply for the integrity of the story. It may be a lifestyle piece for Thanksgiving that needs verification of exactly what the Pilgrims ate that first Thanksgiving Day (it wasn't turkey!). It may be a piece on illegal immigration into Texas that requires data on the number of aliens crossing illegally into Texas in the past ten years. The number of different Barbie doll editions, the year the Edsel automobile came on the market, and the exact age of the pope are all possible research topics.

News Researcher. City newspaper. Work with reporters to acquire and analyze government databases for enterprise, breaking news, and investigative reporting. Desired skills: Foxpro, Excel, MapInfo, Cold Fusion.

---

continued

> **Research Analyst.** Canada's largest circulation newspaper is looking for an experienced researcher with database skills. Help obtain data for newspaper stories and analyze the information. Must be proficient in building and querying relational databases and spreadsheets. Experience with freedom of information requests is an asset.
>
> **Junior Investigative Researcher.** Law firm. Undertake public records research and retrieval. Conduct reliable evaluations of information that is retrieved. Requires working knowledge of research applications including LexisNexis, Edgar, and Internet sources, and also Microsoft products. Must possess strong organizational, communication, and analytical skills.

Working Conditions. Far more creative than many would give credit for, researching is the investigative art used in the world of words. Developing leads, exhausting false trails, and running a fact or thematic possibility to ground can be exciting when you realize your provision of materials through research can ultimately affect the production of a piece of text. Most researchers tend to be experienced in certain specific areas, but their skills are highly transferable, and some are able to freelance for a variety of information users.

Both fiction and nonfiction writers buy research services. For example, a novelist might set a wedding scene in Fiji that is critical to the book but not very long. Nonfiction writers may need background on real events or people in history. And prose writers are not the researcher's only clients; advertising agencies, television reporters, newspapers, historical societies and museums, and private individuals also have needs for research work.

Training and Qualifications. A high level of general knowledge, curiosity, persistence, perseverance, and attention to detail are salient qualifications of a researcher. Caring about written text, facts, and accuracy is crucial. Very often, researchers have little to go on as they begin their quest for information, so they must be resourceful and efficient in their work.

Perhaps you've been assigned to do research for a film set in the 1960s. There is continuing interest in some of the cultural, social, and political effects of the sixties. President John F. Kennedy, Marilyn Monroe, the Beatles, and Vietnam are still very much with us as touchstones of a different time.

You've been asked to help evoke this era by researching food trends. You discover in your research an emphasis on packaged foods. Americans had just discovered biscuits in a can, cake mixes, gelatin desserts, casseroles made with canned soup, and a host of other culinary delights (which thankfully have not all survived into the present). You've read newspapers and cookbooks and talked to homemakers who used these products. Your research leads you to contact some of the manufacturers who are still operating, and you discover a treasure trove of recipes, photographs, and even films of kitchens, table settings, and menus—more than you had expected it would be possible to dig up.

Perhaps some of what you discover even links with some of the material that is being developed. You locate a film, with sound, of a teen party that effectively shows off clothing, party food, behavior, and musical selections that proves invaluable to the art director for the film.

Earnings. Because the researcher can work in so many different settings and have many different job titles, salaries will vary widely. To get some sense for salary potential, visit salaryexpert.com, enter a job title, for example "market research analyst," and a geographic location, and you will be shown current salary information. Newly degreed researchers working for the federal government would start at Grade 7, for which the minimum salary listed in the federal government's Annual Salary Table 2005 General Schedule is $30,567.

Creative Writing

When we think of creative writing, we think immediately of the novelist, but creative writing is far more than that. It includes lyricists, songwriters, and poets. It is the work of those who write from their own inspiration (many would substitute *perspiration*) and who feel strongly the need to express in writing their own view of the world, be it in song, verse, or prose. There certainly exist employers who hire creative writers, but the overwhelming majority are self-employed as writers, although they may have a "day job" to support their writing efforts.

Working Conditions. The eternal juggling act of balancing the need for income with the desire to write exerts tremendous pressure on creative writers. Many must use early-morning or late-night hours to do what they consider their "real" work of expressing themselves through words. Until they are able to support themselves by their writing, many work at jobs and schedules that, although perhaps not the best use of their talents, will allow them the freedom and time to write. Their writing is solitary work, often done under less than ideal conditions.

For example, Dr. Perri Klass, an active Boston obstetrician, wife, and mother, as well as a prolific knitter and designer, somehow maintains the production of a fluid stream of articles, magazine pieces, and books. Do a Web search for "Perri Klass" and you are certain to turn up reviews of her books, schedules of her speaking engagements, and audio clips from her national lecture tours.

Even acknowledging that some people have more energy than others, this kind of production speaks of a determined schedule of sitting down and doing the writing. The increments of time may not be as luxurious as a full-time writer can afford, but they are dedicated, honored moments set aside to write.

There is an excellent array of published materials to help the creative writer break into this field. These books include the current year's *Writer's Market*, *Poet's Market*, *Song Writer's Market*, and *Novel and Short Story Writer's Market*. Many college career offices and public libraries contain recent editions of these volumes. Each provides specific information on how to target your efforts and how to contact potential publishers. They also contain articles and interviews with top professional writers.

Training and Qualifications. Because so much of this work is independent and solitary, the qualifications here are simply the desire and compulsion to write and express oneself. However, close behind these primary qualifications are the ability to tolerate risk in a profession with no guarantees, the poise and equanimity to stick with a job for the income to support your writing, and a saleable skill to keep you employed until you have your first break with a publication.

Most of all, the independent writer needs self-discipline. We have said that many work at home during "fringe time"—late at night or early in the morning. Many have written about the struggle to maintain such a difficult schedule. Over and over again, the successful writer will be the self-disciplined writer who learns to stick to a schedule and accomplish something each day. Writers must see their writing as something that they do regardless of how they feel that day, of what problems or concerns have arisen, or of fine weather that may tempt them out of doors. They must stick to a schedule, whether of time or number of pages. In this way, they produce, and without that self-discipline they will have no product to present to the reading public.

Earnings. Unlike any other of the career paths discussed in this book, the earnings of the self-employed creative writer tend to be accretive: success builds on success, and usually published work begets published work. The artist or sculptor may set a price for a creation, but most writers will tell you that until they achieve some fame, the pricing for their efforts is established by the buyer.

There are writers who sell their work literally by the word, and others receive a flat fee for a work. Many magazines and journals issue lists indicating what they pay for unsolicited work. One excellent source providing current pricing information for hundreds of creative writing opportunities is the latest edition of *Writer's Market*. Online, visit writersweekly.com to see freelance job listings and what they pay. Professional fee guidelines for writers in Canada can be found at writers.ca/whattopay.htm.

Career Outlook

According to the U.S. Department of Labor, Bureau of Labor Statistics (BLS), employment of reporters is expected to grow more slowly than the average for all occupations through the year 2012. The BLS cites mergers and consolidation in the newspaper industry, increasing expenses, decreasing circulation, and declines in advertising profits as the reasons for this slower growth. The outlook for writers and editors is a bit better—employment is expected to grow about as fast as the average for all occupations through the year 2012.

Even with increased competition in the economy, bachelor's degree holders who want to work as market research analysts will vie for a limited number of jobs. Your best bet is to look for research assistant positions with private firms.

To gain an employer's attention as you apply for positions, you must very clearly indicate in your cover letter and résumé what relevant skills you have to offer, the experience you can bring to the table, and how you can help accomplish the goals of the employing organization.

The creative writer should take heart. We have an ever-increasing number of magazine editions for every taste and a burgeoning entertainment industry that is always looking for creative and original material. The career path of the creative writer is seldom secure and never guaranteed, but as long as media and vehicles for publishing continue to exist and thrive, there will be opportunities.

Technology has changed the face of the publishing industry. Although most industry experts say they do not believe the book as a publishing format will ever disappear, some individuals say that interactive media will replace books as the number of people comfortable with using various kinds of hardware and software increases. Available products, ways of doing business, and new job titles in the writing field, such as electronic publishing specialist, will continue to alter the face of editing and publishing as the industry embraces ever-changing technologies.

Desktop publishing has allowed many writers and editors with graphics ability to develop businesses producing pamphlets, brochures, informational pieces, booklets, and electronic (digital) layouts for any number of small publishing ventures. This kind of activity will continue to increase and reduce the obstacles to small-scale publishing.

One of the technical changes for writers, scholars, reporters, and editors has been the availability of data due to the computer's ability to store and retrieve data in response to various modes of inquiry. This proliferation of data means work for researchers, especially researchers skilled in the latest technology. Not only must researchers know how to find data, but they need to be able to create their own databases for their professional files and future reference.

Although the number of daily newspapers continues to decline, the availability of news electronically requires writers, researchers, and editors. Television promises to become more interactive and specialized. Cable television channels offer twenty-four-hour news programs that use substantial editorial and writing staffs, and we are seeing increasing numbers of programs devoted to news, features, health, business, international affairs, and senior citizen issues.

Strategy for Finding the Jobs

As we stated previously, competition for these types of jobs is stiff. However, undertaking the three tasks described below will give you a leg up on other job seekers.

Decide What Interests You and Focus on It

The preceding section is dramatic evidence that the opportunities in writing, editing, and publishing are both vast and diverse. Although traditional areas of employment such as editing and publishing may be oversubscribed, we have outlined other clusters of potential jobs. Where to begin? Begin with your strengths, energies, and enthusiasm. Simply put, select one of the possible employment areas that interests and motivates you most (such as specialized publications, broadcasting, or newspapers) and focus your initial efforts on that sector.

Create a Specialized List of Employers

You have already developed a list of job titles. Now, using the suggested employer contacts we have provided, begin to develop a full list of potential employers in the field you are targeting. Don't stop with the material provided in this text. Use the Internet, your local library, chamber of commerce, and college career center for additional employers. Perhaps your college can put you in touch with alumni who are already employed in the field you are interested in who will be willing to help you with employment information.

Use All Your Experience

Perhaps, as you work through your list, you'll discover you need more technical background than you now have for a particular writing or publishing field. Or it may be that the economy has had a negative impact on one of these areas and hiring for new positions is frozen. If, after some investigation and interviewing, you decide to move on to a different employment sector where possibilities seem greater, your initial efforts are not wasted. The research skills you've employed, the contacts you've made, and the relationships you've established with helpful professionals will serve only to enhance and speed your activity in a new direction.

Possible Employers

As you begin to develop a list of employers that offer jobs in writing, editing, and publishing, you'll see there are many possibilities. You might, for example, be interested in working in news writing because, after all, we all want to have some level of awareness about what's going on in the world. If you read a daily newspaper, you probably glance at the headlines before you leave home for the day. You may flip on the TV to see what's happened overnight. News readers fill you in on the latest. Or you may have a very hectic schedule and catch up on the news by going online during a break or at lunchtime. No matter how you get your news, someone is writing it, editing it, and presenting it via one medium or another.

We will begin to explore possible employers by examining some of the media used in writing, editing, and publishing. These include newspapers;

general circulation magazines; trade, technical, and professional publications; agricultural newspapers and magazines; targeted population publications; college and university newspapers and magazines; radio stations; TV stations; cable TV systems; book publishers; academic presses; and government.

Newspapers

There are almost 1,500 daily newspapers available in the United States, and about 100 daily newspapers in Canada. All these newspapers employ hundreds of thousands of workers. More than 1,500 of these papers have launched websites. Each one of these print and/or Internet newspapers is available because a group of people, some of whom have skills similar to those you possess, has worked together to get the written word out.

While the principal role of the daily newspaper has been to provide stories and background on local, regional, state, and national events, situations, and concerns as they occur, newspapers have become increasingly diversified. Many now have extensive indexes directing the public to sections on lifestyle, science and health, business, home and family, and entertainment. All of this has been designed to entice a larger and broader-based audience and to enculturate a younger generation to the rewards of daily newspaper reading. Because of the sheer number of newspapers being published, they continue to be a large employer of people interested in writing, editing, and publishing.

Help in Locating These Employers. If you would like to identify the newspapers currently in business in a particular area, several resources will be helpful: Newspapers.com (newspapers.com) lists newspapers by state with links to websites and also has links to well-known sites that list jobs. *Editor and Publisher International Yearbook*, a resource you might find at your college or larger local library, lists contact information for U.S. and Canadian daily newspapers. Be sure to review the book *Careers in Journalism* or the *Gale Directory of Publications and Broadcast Media* as well.

Some excellent resources for gaining additional information about the newspaper industry include the Newspaper Association of America (naa.org); National Newspaper Association (nna.org); and *Editor and Publisher* (editorandpublisher.com). Each website has links that will be extremely useful in your job search.

General Circulation Magazines

Almost nineteen thousand consumer magazines are available in North America. These publications cover a range of interests from alternative, underground, and New Age to business, soccer, and youth. There are fashion magazines for infants, for men, and for women over forty. There are craft magazines for every conceivable hobby and an equally broad array of specialized sport enthusiast publications. A new and growing segment is a range of magazine publications for young people age twenty to twenty-five with editorial content, advertisements, and graphics that speak distinctly to this target market.

Each publication offers staff positions in the areas of writing, editing, researching, graphics, and thematic planning. There is also a considerable market for freelance article writers on every subject.

Help in Locating These Employers. For more information about this industry, review *Folio: The Magazine for Magazine Management*, the *Gale Directory of Publications and Broadcast Media*, the *National Directory of Magazines*, Standard Rate and Data Service publications, and Publishers Information Bureau publications.

Trade, Technical, and Professional Newspapers and Magazines

If you have ever examined the *Encyclopedia of Associations*, a four-volume set, you realize how many American nonprofit membership organizations there are. Tens of thousands of organizations are listed in this encyclopedia. You will see entries for nearly any type of organization you can imagine, from the National Institute of Benefits Administrators to the Psychic Rescue Squad, the Strategy Gaming Society, and the Swedish Chamber of Commerce of the U.S.A. Each of these organizations serves a specific purpose and accomplishes for its members what those members individually would not be able to do. One of the principal missions of this type of organization is education of the organization's members, and nearly every association publishes at least one informational piece. This is often a directory of members or an annual report, or it may be a brochure outlining the organization's members, goals, and mission. Staff sizes range from one person to several hundred people, and larger organizations employ individuals specifically to write, edit, and publish.

A visit to a succession of business employers, from the largest and most sophisticated of corporations to the smallest of warehouse operations, would dramatically demonstrate the size and pervasiveness of the trade publication sector. On coffee tables in each of these organizations you would find on display beautiful publications that rival any in the commercial marketplace, the subjects ranging from industrial boilers to commercial food products. All contain photography, graphics, color work, editorial comment, and freelance articles. Contrary to popular belief, such publications do not contain only highly technical information, either. There are humorous articles, philosophical pieces, critical commentary, and futuristic writing. Many English majors who have found a home in the trade publishing industry make a strong case for the quality and creativity of these publications.

Help in Locating These Employers. Currently, there are thousands of publications that are classified as trade, technical, and professional newspapers and magazines, and you'll find them being published in nearly every state. The *Gale Directory of Publications and Broadcast Media* is an excellent resource for locating publications either by subject area or by geographic location. The *Encyclopedia of Associations* also lists the publications each professional organization makes available. Most professional organizations and associations maintain websites. Given the huge number of associations and the publications they make available, this is an employment possibility that should not be overlooked.

Agricultural Newspapers and Magazines

The United States is fortunate to have a variety of soil types, climates, and resources that support a great diversity of agricultural production. In this country alone there are hundreds of publications that relate to agriculture: research, livestock production, and so on. Some of the larger publications relating to this industry include *Progressive Farmer*, *Western Horseman*, *Successful Farming*, and *Agribusiness: An International Journal*.

Agricultural publications represent the history and diversity of farming and the changes the agricultural industry has undergone as it moves from a labor-intensive to a technologically intensive business. Nevertheless, agriculture remains one of the most challenging and frustrating areas of commercial endeavor, due in large part to the impact of the weather. The publications that support agriculture are indicative of those concerns, with articles and columns ranging from country cooking to the most sophisticated farming technology advice. There are interviews, biographies, historical articles, and pictorials. Be sure to obtain some copies of such publications and review them. You may be surprised at the content and delighted to find you could make a contribution.

Help in Locating These Employers. If you have a special interest in agriculture in addition to writing, editing, and publishing, it is easy to identify these publications using the *Gale Directory of Publications and Broadcast Media* or *Business Rankings Annual*. Then check the Internet for publications' websites.

A few of the larger professional associations that provide information and also produce publications themselves include the American Society for Horticultural Science (ashs.org), American Farm Bureau (fb.com), and Horticulture Research International (hridir.org).

Targeted-Population Newspapers and Magazines

One exciting change in publishing has come about with the United States' growing awareness and appreciation of our multicultural heritage. We are valuing and learning about this cultural pluralism in schools, festivals, on college campuses, and in cities and towns around the country. Communities of ethnic, cultural, racial, and gender-oriented populations are increasingly producing written materials to communicate with each other and with the general public.

These publications resist easy classification and may be found under a number of different headings in various directories. These newspapers and magazines reach out to such populations as African-Americans, foreign language speakers, members of fraternal organizations, lesbians and gay men, Hispanics, Jews, members of religious groups, and women. There are almost eight hundred publications that serve these various groups. Titles of just a few of these newspapers and magazines include *Columbia Black News, Afro-American Times, China Daily News, M.S.U. Alumni Magazine, Hispanic USA Magazine, The Jewish Herald, Gender and Society, Gay Community News,* and *Feminist Bookstore News.*

Help in Locating These Employers. Each one of these newspapers and magazines requires a staff of qualified people to bring it to publication. If you are particularly interested in working with one of these targeted publications, develop a list of potential employers by reviewing resources such as *Burrelle's Media Directory* or *Gale Directory of Publications and Broadcast Media.* Many of these potential employers maintain a website that lists employment opportunities, so use your favorite search engine to find these sites on the Internet.

College and University Newspapers and Magazines

Nearly every college and university produces a student newspaper and at least one alumni newsletter or magazine. In the United States there are almost one thousand such publications. At smaller institutions, a faculty member advises students working on the newspaper, and alumni publications are written by staff working in the alumni office. At larger schools, however, there are specific positions involving writing, editing, and publishing.

Working with a publication dedicated to an audience such as college alumni means you are writing for an educated, sophisticated audience. Indiana University's alumni magazine, for example, is a glossy magazine that runs almost seventy-five pages. Along with the usual class notes and advertisements for college logo products, it carries stimulating articles on art, athletics, and psychological issues as well as alumni profiles. Production values are competitive with most commercial publications.

Help in Locating These Employers. Two sources that will help you to identify potential employers are the *Chronicle of Higher Education* (chronicle.com), which lists actual job openings, and the *Gale Directory of Publications and Broadcast Media*, which lists the schools that publish these types of newspapers and magazines.

Two associations that are worth contacting are College Media Advisors (collegemedia.org) and the Council for Advancement and Support of Education (case.org).

Radio Stations

Radio, which includes both AM and FM stations, is the most pervasive of all media. Nearly every household and vehicle on the street, and even many people walking or running, use a radio to get news, listen to favorite music, or find out about emergency situations. There are more than nine thousand radio stations in the United States employing people who write and edit for the listening public.

Radio provides wonderful opportunities to write for the spoken word. Commercials, intros, bridges, commentaries, news, and weather provide excellent opportunities to practice the writer's craft. Some of this, depending on the size of the station, is done under pressure of time and may lack editorial control. Smaller stations can prove to be valuable entries into writing careers in the public media.

Help in Locating These Employers. If you would like to find out which broadcasting and Web radio stations are based in a given geographic location, check shgresources.com/resources/radio or your library's copy of the *Gale Directory of Publications and Broadcast Media*.

Professional societies that can provide additional information about working in radio include the National Association of Broadcasters (nab.org), Radio-Television News Directors Association (rtnda.org), and the International Radio and Television Society (irts.org).

Television Stations

Although many jobs in broadcast television are available at commercial stations, the biggest being ABC, NBC, and CBS, there are also a number of independent, cable, corporate, and government television stations throughout the United States. There are more than one thousand television stations operating, each of which provides job opportunities for people interested in writing and editing.

Local stations and affiliates provide a feeder system of professionals to the major stations, and there is considerable movement between employers in this industry. Moves are usually indicative of increased responsibility, salary, and professional development, so frequent job movement does not have the stigma that it might in some other industries. In fact, it is often seen in a positive light.

Help in Locating These Employers. Some sources that can be used to identify television stations include the website shgresources.com/resources/tv, the National Association of Broadcasters website (nab.org), and *AV Marketplace*.

Cable Systems

The cable television industry now counts almost nine thousand systems in use. The proliferation of competing cable companies, each offering its own package of systems and fees, has prompted intense public and government scrutiny. These firms, originally behind the scenes, now frequently find themselves in public forums and needing to produce more and more informational material for a market demanding quality and pricing standards. As this industry grows, the opportunities in writing, editing, and publishing will increase proportionately.

Help in Locating These Employers. If you visit Multichannel News online (multichannel.com) and navigate to the Resources tab, you will find links to cable networks and industry association websites. The *Gale Directory of Publications and Broadcast Media* will also help you identify potential employers. If you would like more information on working in cable television, contact the National Cable and Telecommunications Association (ncta.com) or the Canadian Cable Television Association (ccta.ca/index.asp).

Book Publishers

This category of employer includes publishers of books for the general reader (both adults and children), textbooks, and paperbacks. Hundreds of publishers are listed in *Writer's Market*, an excellent reference for those interested in writing, editing, and publishing.

For many English majors, book publishing remains a glamour industry, at least in image. The competition and attractiveness of the profession suggest that only the most aggressive and talented candidates will meet the increasingly demanding criteria for quality employees in an industry that is becoming leaner.

Help in Locating These Employers. Some excellent resources for identifying publishing houses include *Opportunities in Publishing Careers*, the current edition of *Writer's Market*, *Literary Marketplace*, and the news magazine of book publishing, *Publishers Weekly* (publishersweekly.com).

Several associations can provide additional information on the book publishing industry. A few examples include the Association of American Publishers (publishers.org), Newsletter and Electronic Publishers Association (newsletters.org), and the Small Publishers Association of North America (spannet.org).

University Presses

University presses are the publishing division primarily of the large research universities. The tradition of university presses, which started at Oxford University in 1478, continues today. These presses serve scholars by disseminating information critical to scholarship and spreading ideas necessary to the academic community. There are more than one hundred member presses in the industry association.

University presses have transformed themselves from their beginnings as a simple expedient of large academic institutions needing in-house production for scholarly material to contenders as major publishing houses bringing high-quality publications to commercial success with the general public through aggressive marketing and distribution.

Help in Locating These Employers. If you are interested in finding out more about this type of publisher, examine the *Gale Directory of Publications and Broadcast Media* or contact the Association of American University Presses (aaupnet.org).

Federal Government

Several federal agencies specifically hire English majors because of the specialized background these degree holders bring with them. These agencies include the Federal Trade Commission (ftc.gov), Department of Labor (dol.gov), National Archives and Records Administration (archives.gov), Research and Special Programs Administration (rspa.dot.gov), and the Department of Commerce's General Services Administration (gsa.gov) and Government Printing Office (gpo.gov).

Help in Locating These Employers. A good place to start looking for actual job listings is on the U.S. government's jobs website (usajobs.opm.gov). This site explains the federal employment process and lets you look at current job openings, get general information on federal agencies, and submit an online application.

If you select the option "Search Jobs" and then "Agency Job Search," you can enter the agency name in the keyword search box, complete other appropriate search items, and then submit your search. A list of job openings will appear on your screen. Select any of the entries to obtain a detailed job description, including information on whom to contact for more information and how to apply for the specific position.

Possible Job Titles

There is a multitude of job titles associated with working in writing, editing, and publishing. Use the *Dictionary of Occupational Titles*, published by the U.S. Department of Labor (occupationalinfo.org), to get a generic description for the particular job titles that interest you the most.

Assignment editor
Assistant editor
Associate editor
Associate news director
Author
Book editor
Bureau reporter
City editor
Columnist
Continuity writer
Copyeditor
Copy writer
Correspondent

Critic
Desk assistant
Dictionary editor
Editorial assistant
Editorial writer
Electronic publishing specialist
External publications editor
Freelance reporter
Ghostwriter
Greeting card writer
Indexer
Internal publications editor
Journalist
Lyricist
News editor
News writer
Newspaper editor
Playwright
Poet
Program proposals coordinator
Publications editor
Reporter
Researcher
Scriptwriter
Senior editor
Speechwriter
Story editor
Stringer
Technical editor
Technical publications writer
Wire editor
Writer

Related Occupations

The excellent communication skills that have led to your interest in working in writing, editing, and publishing are also valued in many other settings. Some positions directly relating to the media we have discussed include radio or television announcer, account director, account coordinator, assistant planner, creative director, media supervisor, production assistant, communications officer, public relations manager, technical writer, fund-raiser, lobbyist, traffic manager, marketing manager, or teacher.

Three words that can be used to describe the personality traits that many writers possess are artistic, enterprising, and social. These traits are also shared by many people who work as furniture designers, narrators, contestant coordinators, auctioneers, magicians, dance instructors, music teachers, and intelligence specialists.

Professional Associations for Writers, Editors, and Publishers

Review each of the associations listed below to see if any of them are of interest to you. Consider joining a group that serves the career area you are interested in. The career benefits these associations provide, such as job listings online or in a journal or newsletter, are available only to members of the group.

American Book Producers Association
160 Fifth Ave.
New York, NY 10010
abpaonline.org
Members/Purpose: Book-producing companies that develop the concepts
    for books; purpose is to increase the book industry's awareness of
    members' capabilities and the state of the book producers' art
Training: Offers workshops
Journals/Publications: Online directory of members, newsletter

American Medical Publishers' Association
14 Fort Hill Rd.
Huntington, NY 11743
ampaonline.org
Members/Purpose: U.S. medical publishing companies; objectives are to
    exchange information among members; to improve the creation,
    distribution, and sale of medical books and journals; to facilitate
    communication with medical organizations, schools, and the medical
    community

Training: Provides ongoing educational programs
Journals/Publications: Quarterly newsletter, directory
Job Listings: Available positions shown in Careers section

American Society of Journalists and Authors
1501 Broadway, Suite 302
New York, NY 10036
asja.org
Members/Purpose: Freelance writers of nonfiction magazine articles and
books
Training: Offers conferences and workshops
Journal/Publication: *ASJA Monthly* newsletter

American Society of Magazine Editors
919 Third Ave.
New York, NY 10022
magazine.org/editorial
Members/Purpose: Professional organization for editors of consumer
magazines and business publications that are edited, published, and sold
in the United States
Training: Offers conferences, seminars, and roundtable luncheons
Journal/Publication: Fact sheets available online
Job Listings: Job bank link on website

American Society of Newspaper Editors
11690B Sunrise Valley Dr.
Reston, VA 20191-1409
asne.org
Members/Purpose: Daily newspaper editors, people who serve the editorial
needs of daily newspapers, and certain distinguished individuals who
have worked on behalf of editors through the years
Training: Hosts convention
Journal/Publication: *The American Editor*
Job Listings: Newspaper Job Resources page links to multiple job listings

Association of American Publishers
71 Fifth Ave.
New York, NY 10003-3004
publishers.org
Members/Purpose: Trade association representing producers of hardbound
and softbound general, educational, trade, reference, religious, scientific,

technical, and medical books; instructional materials; classroom periodicals; maps, globes, tests, and software

Training: Conducts seminars and workshops on various publishing topics including rights and permission, sales, and educational publishing

Job Listings: BookJobs links to available positions

The Authors Guild
31 E. 28th St., 10th Floor
New York, NY 10016-7923
authorsguild.org
Members/Purpose: Professional organization of authors of books, magazine material, and plays
Journals/Publications: *Author's Guild Bulletin*, quarterly review

Canadian Newspaper Association
890 Yonge St., Suite 200
Toronto, ON M4W 3P4
Canada
cna-acj.ca
Members/Purpose: Represents the needs of its members and the public in the areas of public policy, marketing, and member services
Training: Offers seminars and workshops
Journal/Publication: *The Press and the Courts*
Job Listings: Links to job postings on website

Magazine Publishers of America
810 Seventh Ave., 24th Floor
New York, NY 10019
magazine.org
Members/Purpose: Represents more than 240 domestic publishing companies with approximately 1,400 titles, more than 80 international companies, and more than 100 associate members
Training: Offers events and seminars
Job Postings: Links to job postings on website

**National Academy of Television Arts
and Sciences**
111 W. 57th St., Suite 1020
New York, NY 10019
emmyonline.org

Members/Purpose: Persons engaged in television performing, art directing, cinematography, directing, taping, tape editing, choreography, engineering, film editing, music, production, and writing
Training: Sponsors workshops and seminars
Journals/Publications: *National News, Television Quarterly*
Job Listings: Can search NATAS job database online

National Association of Broadcasters
1771 N St. NW
Washington, DC 20036
nab.org
Members/Purpose: Representatives of radio and television stations and television networks; associate members include producers of equipment and programs
Training: Hosts convention and meetings
Job Listings: Online career center lists job openings

Newspaper Association of America
1921 Gallows Rd., Suite 600
Vienna, VA 22182-3900
naa.org
Members/Purpose: Represents the newspaper industry and more than two thousand newspapers in the United States and Canada
Training: Hosts conferences and meetings
Journal/Publication: *Presstime*
Job Listings: Links to job postings on website

Society of National Association Publications
8405 Greensboro Dr., #800
McLean, VA 22102
snaponline.org
Members/Purpose: Publications owned, operated, or controlled by voluntary associations and societies, including organizations with licensing and certification functions
Training: Sponsors seminars and resource networks
Journal/Publication: *Association Publishing* magazine
Job Listings: Online Career Center contains links to job listings

Path 2: Teaching

Talk to any English teachers you know, and they'll tell you a surprising fact about the teaching profession. They don't teach English, they teach students! The art of teaching and the skill required in the dynamics of student interaction weigh far more heavily in this equation than love of or interest in the subject matter. The subject might be English, but the overriding concerns in this profession are conveying an appreciation of English in all its forms of expression to learners who come to the classroom with different issues, at different ages, from different lifestyles, and with dramatically different degrees of interest in the subject. With all that in the way, simply loving English yourself is not enough, although that is certainly important and desirable. How could you teach something you didn't truly enjoy and expect not to convey that lack of interest through a mechanical approach to the subject?

Teaching is a unique art and demands skills you probably didn't acquire in your studies of English. These skills have very little to do with your own proficiency in the subject. The world is full of skillful practitioners who, for one reason or another and often inexplicably, cannot teach someone how they do what they do. The practice of something is very different from professing it in a classroom.

For example, planning for learning outcomes is critical. Teaching English within an established curriculum may mean corresponding to state educational goals for high schools or a course outline in a college catalog. To accomplish this body of learning within a set time requires judicious planning of the material. What will be done each day? How much time will you allow between assignments or readings? Which materials will you require and which will you only recommend? Scores of decisions must be made about how material will be introduced, presented, and ultimately delivered back to you for evaluation.

Add to this the fact that students learn in different ways. Some are auditory learners who enjoy listening and gain most of their information in this way. If they are required to take notes while listening, something may have to give, and it may be difficult for them to retain the material. For others, auditory learning is less successful, and they prefer a visual approach with board work, handouts, their own notes, diagrams, books, and many visual materials. Visual learners retain these images and can call them up to remember the material.

Others learn best by participating through reading in class, performing, team projects, and other activities that physically involve them. These are kinesthetic learners, and they are often forgotten in curriculum design and lesson planning. Professional teachers ensure that their classes satisfy the learning styles of all their students through judicious combinations of modalities in teaching. The professional teacher has analyzed his or her own teaching style and seeks to incorporate the elements that come less naturally to maximize learning by every student.

The teaching and learning that takes place in a class is not static. The classroom is an emotionally charged environment for the student and instructor that may call into play questions of self-esteem and competency. People are exploring new definitions of themselves in relation to their capabilities, values, or achievement. A good teacher understands this and encourages a risk-free environment of mutual appreciation and participation. Both teacher and student are allowed to make mistakes and move on. The teacher strives to assist in establishing congruence between the self (who we know we are right now), the ideal self (who we want to be), and the learning environment created in the classroom. The classroom should be a place where our real selves can rise up and begin to touch our ideal selves.

Any mention of competency, self-esteem, or self-worth naturally suggests the subject of grading and the evaluation teachers provide. Grades are an expected and required part of many institutional academic settings. Establishing fair and consistent standards of evaluating students and assigning grades is a significant challenge to many teachers who otherwise feel perfectly competent in the teaching role. English teachers particularly find that grading the numerous required essays is highly subjective, and they are always seeking better ways to ensure fairness in grading this kind of assignment. Students often complain about grading practices in teachers they, in every other respect, feel positive about.

The teacher of English is called on to play other roles, too. Animating the class and inspiring attention and commitment to the material are all required in teaching. Part of this is the teacher's enthusiasm, part is teaching style, and part is effective use of ancillary materials and the ability to relate this material to a student's life. English teachers, of course, present information and demonstrate periods, schools, and styles of particular writers or poets. They seek to raise relevant questions, prompt dialogues in the class, and develop in students the discipline of self-questioning. They clarify difficulties or obscurities in the material and draw parallels or find relationships between examples.

For a professional teacher, each class is not only an opportunity to teach the subject, English, but to teach students how to learn as well. How to question, how to record information, how to be selective, and how to retain information are ongoing lessons that take place in every classroom to some degree.

A good teacher also uses the class and the material to explain how this material reflects feelings. A teacher will share his or her own agreement with or support of ideas or emotions in the material under study. Most of all, an instructor will evaluate and by example develop the student's capacity for self-evaluation through careful, caring feedback about both in-class and out-of-class work. The instructor's own example of preparation, organization, personal appearance, evaluation standards, interest in his or her students, and enthusiasm will remain an example long after the memory of the actual class content has faded.

Teachers are frequently cited as important factors in students' choice of a career. Teachers themselves often remember one or two of their own teachers who were strong influences on their decision to teach. Much of that influence is a result of teachers' presence in the classroom. They serve as models of people enjoying what they are doing and doing it skillfully. They are professional yet remained natural and approachable. Students watch and listen to them and think, "Maybe I could do that."

Definition of the Career Path

We'll look at two possible levels of teaching English: secondary school teaching with a bachelor's degree and college teaching, possibly with a master's degree but more frequently requiring a doctoral degree as the essential credential.

Following graduation, certified secondary school teachers apply for advertised positions in public high schools. Teaching positions are well advertised, and all certified teacher graduates are qualified for entry-level English teaching assignments. Usually advertisements for public school positions do not contain a lot of information. On the other hand, private/independent schools generally provide detailed information in their ads. These two recent postings are typical:

Education—Teacher. Regional school district in Connecticut. To teach English grades 9–12. Interested applicants are asked to send a letter of intent, résumé, copies of transcripts and certification, and three letters of recommendation.

High School English Teacher. We are seeking a full-time high school English teacher to begin immediately, preferably with a specialty in British literature. The job includes four sections of eleventh grade British literature, one of which is advanced placement, one honors, and two standard sections. This is a position at a prestigious independent school with relatively small classes and motivated students. Master's recommended. Please visit our website for more information about our school, and call/e-mail us for information on how to apply.

Is it possible to teach English at the high school level without state certification and with a bachelor of arts in English? Yes, in some public school districts that have had difficulty securing teachers because of location or pay scales, provisions have been made to grant temporary certification to non-credentialed teachers. This is, however, not very common. Some private high schools also might consider a noncertified teacher, but private schools increasingly do require teaching preparation that equals or is very close to that which public schools require. In fact, at some private schools, it is not uncommon for a majority of the English teachers to have master's degrees, and numerous large city high schools have attracted Ph.D.s as well.

A master's degree in English literature may be helpful in securing a private school teaching position at the high school level, especially if the master's specialty work in English corresponds to the school's needs, for example twentieth-century British literature or early-nineteenth-century American writers.

Graduates with master's degrees and no certification at the bachelor's level may also find employment in junior and community college settings or special college programs for adult learners. These schools may also welcome the teacher with a master's degree, especially if the specialty is one that corresponds to the curriculum. The following is an actual advertisement for a college-level English instructor with a master's degree:

English Faculty Position. College offers two-year degree programs. Responsibilities: teach college English courses, advise students, participate in college committees and projects, participate in community activities, and continue professional growth. Requires master's degree in English with at least eighteen graduate semester hours or quarter hours in the discipline, one or more graduate courses in composition studies, experience teaching English composition, commitment to the teaching/learning process in a two-year community college, and willingness to use technology for classroom instruction.

The doctoral degree in English opens up the world of college teaching to the prospective educator. Positions are well advertised in vehicles such as the *Chronicle of Higher Education* (chronicle.com), a weekly newspaper that reports on higher education issues and contains the most complete list available of faculty, staff, and leadership position openings for colleges and universities in the United States and some foreign countries. The following is an ad from the Chronicle that would be of interest to a new Ph.D. in English:

Assistant Professor of English. Tenure track in American multicultural literature. Area of specialization should be in one or more of the following: African-American literature, Latina/o or Chicana/o literature, Native American literature, Asian-American literature, or ethnic literature. Requires excellence in teaching and scholarship, as well as involvement in college and departmental service. Course load is three classes per semester. Teach surveys, specialty courses, and at least one composition course per year. Minimum qualifications: ABD in English at time of application with doctorate to be completed by August 15, 200_, plus teaching experience at college or university level with documentation of teaching success.

This ad is interesting—it allows ABD (all but dissertation) candidates to apply, but requires completion of the degree within nine months of being hired. An earned doctorate will pay more than an ABD and will lead more directly and quickly to possible tenure and promotion. ABD candidates will also have to decide how they will finish their degree (the dissertation often being the most time-consuming aspect of earning a Ph.D.) while holding down a full-time job.

As is true in this ad, teaching freshman composition classes is generally part of the teaching load of new college English teachers. Many of these students will be taking English composition because it is a college requirement for graduation and not because they are English majors or have chosen the course. The English department performs a service to the entire college in offering this course. Generally, even senior faculty will teach at least one composition class, but as you become more senior in the faculty you can take on courses more directly related to your interests and educational background.

The ad also contains a request for documentation of teaching success. This could come from teaching assistantships done while working on the doctoral degree. Many students acquire this experience as graduate teaching assistants, part-time faculty, lecturers, or adjunct faculty at other colleges or programs.

The advertisement also calls for an area of specialization. This could be substantiated either through a transcript showing course work in one of the areas, published articles or papers on some aspect of the specialization, or recommendations from colleagues stating your expertise in one of the designated areas.

The road to a doctorate is fairly long and arduous. It is hard work. Along the way, you'll meet some wonderful people, some who'll be friends and colleagues the rest of your life. Even colleagues separated by long distances have the opportunity to meet at conferences and symposia. You'll have opportunities to write, teach, and perhaps publish—all before you finish your degree.

Take advantage of these opportunities when you can. As the advertisement shown suggests, some of those kinds of qualifications will be asked of you. However, it is possible to become overly involved in some of these areas to the detriment of degree progress.

There has been considerable discussion in academic circles about the time to degree for students in the humanities. The median time required to complete the Ph.D. after receiving a baccalaureate degree is 11.3 years, and the time taken since starting graduate school is 9 years. For all fields of study, the median number of years to earn a Ph.D. after earning a baccalaureate is 10.1 years, and since starting graduate school is 7.5 years.

The longer time to degree for students in the humanities may have something to do with the more defined parameters of the fields of science. Science places an emphasis on correct process, formula, and execution, whereas in English, some researchers suggest, there seems to be less decision making on the part of advisers, doctoral committees, and other participants about the proper timeline for earning the degree and what needs to be accomplished during that period.

Working Conditions

The working conditions for teachers of English are dramatically different according to the educational setting. The high school English teacher has a full complement of classes, perhaps as many as five or six a day, and may have study hall or lunchroom supervision duties during the week, responsibility for an after-school detention center, or even a sports activity to supervise. Discipline has a major impact in the secondary classroom and is perhaps the single most dominant element of the working conditions for the secondary English teacher. Because the student population in large part is not voluntary, resistance is prevalent and acting out through poor discipline and bad behavior is common.

The effective classroom teacher is one who has successfully mastered classroom management. For many young teachers, these are the most challenging lessons in teaching, and they make for the most interesting stories as teachers grow in their profession. The balance between teaching English and classroom discipline is seldom in equilibrium and can be particularly frustrating, as when one disruptive student threatens the decorum of an otherwise studious class.

Most public high schools have fairly rigid systems for enforcing behavior norms, and the principal agents of that enforcement are the faculty. To elect high school English education as your particular arena is to challenge your ability to maintain your poise and your focus on your subject matter and your interest in training and shaping young people while at the same time administering the disciplinary elements mandated by your school. These sanctions include grades, warnings, parent conferences, detention, dismissal, and referrals to other helping agencies in or out of the school system.

The secondary teacher's workday is a full day with established starting and ending times as well as much at-home work. Perhaps among the busiest of at-home schedules are those of the English faculty. Much of English teachers' work outside the classroom involves writing assignments, and giving the valuable feedback students need on their writing involves hours of reading and providing commentary. Staying ahead of text and book assignments is also time-consuming, as is maintaining required records of attendance, grades, warnings, progress reports, and other evaluation instruments that may be required in your school district.

High school English teachers often take on other assignments as well, such as homeroom duty, field trips, arranging for guest speakers, chaperone duties, and advising activities for yearbooks, literary journals, or clubs in the school. These can demand a great deal of time, and it is important that the teacher entering into secondary English teaching understand that these assignments are a typical part of a high school teaching professional's commitment.

A college teaching environment is significantly different from a high school setting. There is less need to appease a number of outside publics. There is no school board to satisfy; there are no parents or parent-teacher groups. The world of the college classroom is closed to outsiders. It is, in fact, rare to have a class interrupted by anyone outside of the room, so understood is this convention. Academic freedom protects the professors in large part and allows them to express themselves within their class material with far greater pointedness than is the case in high school.

Grading, evaluation procedures, numbers of tests, even the issues of whether to have textbooks and tests are entirely up to the faculty member. If the rationale supports these decisions, the administration does not interfere. An added protection is the granting of tenure to established professors who have documented significant teaching histories and excellent student reviews, publications, campus committee work, and outreach to the community. The granting of tenure gains professors an additional degree of job security and further supports their expression of academic freedom. All of these conditions make the classroom environment and the relations of faculty and students very different than what has come before in the students' education.

The teaching day in a college or university setting involves fewer class hours taught per day and per week. At an institution that focuses on faculty research, the teacher would be responsible for teaching two to three courses that each meet three to four hours per week. Schools that emphasize teaching rather than research require instructors to teach three to four courses for a total of nine to twelve hours of class meetings per week. These class hours and some mandated office hours for advising students are the principal requirements for attendance on the faculty member's part. But as the following ad makes clear, there are other expectations:

> **English Department Tenure-Track Position.** Assistant, tenure track,
> starting fall 200_. Responsibilities: teach courses in English education, supervise
> student teachers, and advise students as a member of a dynamic and growing
> English program committed to excellent undergraduate and post-degree
> education. Minimum qualifications: doctorate in English, English education, or
> equivalent field in hand by August 200_; two years teaching experience; and
> ability to conduct research. Preference will be given to individuals who have
> experience working with student teachers in a supervisory position and
> demonstrate interest in working with a diverse student population.

In addition to courses and advising, scholarly research is an expectation even of those colleges for whom tenure is not based on publication. All colleges want their faculty to contribute to the scholarly dialogue in their discipline, and this is reviewed by chairs of departments and academic deans periodically throughout the instructor's career. It may be a determining element in granting tenure or promotion to a faculty member and may influence issues such as salary negotiations, merit increases, and the like.

Committee work is also important, because the faculty at most colleges are the governing and rule-making bodies who determine and vote on governance and program changes. Committee work can be issue-oriented, such as a commission on the status of women or a pay equity survey; it may be programmatic, such as a committee to study the core curriculum for undergraduates or to devise a new graphic arts major; or it may be related to credentials, as in a committee set up to prepare materials for an accreditation visit.

Some committees are permanent, such as academic standards, curriculum review, promotion and tenure, planning, and administrator review committees, though the members may change on a rotating schedule. Other groups are formed for a limited time or until completion of some task. These committees are essential and are one vehicle for guiding the direction of the school. Having the support of all the faculty and constantly fresh and interested members helps to ensure all voices are heard and many different opinions considered in making what are often far-reaching decisions.

A college day is certainly less rigid than a high school schedule, though it may be just as busy and as long. The difference in content is that for the high school teacher, much of the day and commitment is enforced and required. The college teacher may certainly feel institutional and professional pressure to fulfill certain roles, but exactly how to do that is up to the individual. There will be classes, office hours, meetings, and research work to do. Faculty members may act as advisers to fraternities, sororities, campus newspapers, and clubs, which may also add to their day.

Training and Qualifications

To teach English at the secondary level requires a bachelor's degree, completion of an approved teacher training program, and supervised practice teaching. These are the basic elements required for public teacher licensure. Each of the fifty states and the District of Columbia require licensure of public school teachers. Private schools, on the other hand, do not require licensure of their teachers.

Teacher training programs are well-defined options within the education curriculum of teacher training colleges and universities. They include a teaching practicum in which you would have the opportunity to leave campus and teach actual English classes under a supervising teacher for an academic quarter or semester. Certification in the state granting the licensure is usually part of the degree process and may include the requirement to participate in a national teacher examination process.

There need not be any mysteries surrounding your eligibility for certification in states other than the state in which you originally earn your teaching certificate. The authors of this book have found the simplest solution to be a search of the particular state's Department of Education website. All the information you need is at your fingertips. There is an excellent website (academploy.com/resources.cfm) that has a submenu that, in many cases, links to complete documentation provided by each state. You'll find in searching this site that many states have nonstandard options for certification, and you'll learn which states have reciprocal certification agreements with other states.

Another option for the individual with a degree in English who desires to teach but lacks certification would be to enroll in a conversion program at a college or university. These programs offer an opportunity to add the necessary state-mandated teaching requirements to an existing degree. Depending on your undergraduate degree and whether a change of institution is involved, this could require twelve to eighteen months of academic enrollment and, in some cases, a full two years. A good website to visit is one published by the National Center for Education, ncei.com/state-alt -contact.htm. It links you to each state's contact for alternative teacher certification.

Such conversion programs can also exist independent of a college or university. Some are the product of a consortium of school districts, such as the Upper Valley Teacher Institute in Lebanon, New Hampshire (uvti.org). This unique teacher qualifying program takes individuals with bachelor's degrees, many of whom have had other careers or significant work experience, and places them with master teachers in actual classrooms for a full year. Half the year is at one grade level, and the other half is with another grade. The year includes much independent work and follows a contract established at the start of the year. There may also be a requirement to participate in an associated classroom program to meet state reading certification requirements.

College and university teaching requires a completed doctorate or, in some cases, all but dissertation (ABD). Salary and assignments may be affected, however, by lack of an earned doctorate. In addition to the doctorate, there may be requirements for teaching experience, special depth of research, background in a particular genre or subject area, and some additional competencies. There is almost always the requirement of teaching basic composition classes to first- and second-year students.

Earnings

Secondary school teachers of English are paid according to the same salary schedules as other teachers in their school districts. Salaries across the nation vary depending upon location, which affects cost of living and level of support of education as reflected in the school budget. A salary survey published by the American Federation of Teachers (AFT) on its website (aft.org) at the time of publication showed estimated beginning teacher salaries. Pay ranged from a high of $38,597 in Alaska to a low of $23,790 in Montana. The AFT website is an excellent source of information on all aspects of the teaching profession. Another source of information is the Education Resources Information Center (eric.ed.gov).

In some situations the first-year teacher's inexperience can be a plus. With school budgets under terrific strain, principals, superintendents, and other hiring officials may be more attracted to a relatively inexperienced teacher who will earn a lower salary than to an experienced teacher, perhaps with an advanced degree, who would take a larger proportion of salary funds.

The *Chronicle of Higher Education*'s annual report on faculty salaries for 2004–05 reported that the average faculty salary for English language and literature/letters positions in four-year public institutions was $54,712, and at private institutions was $57,783. Remember that these numbers represent averages for all ranks combined, so starting salaries will be lower, and in some cases much lower, than this. Those who teach in higher education are not drawn to the work because of high pay, but one item to note for those interested in teaching English is that this discipline is among the lowest paid of all the disciplines.

Career Outlook

The career outlook for secondary school teachers of English must take into account the number of baby boomer teachers who will retire, the size of the population of secondary school students, and the geographic location of the school. Generally speaking, opportunities for English teachers are expected to be good through the year 2012, which will require less attractive school districts to offer higher pay, and in some cases signing bonuses, in order to attract teacher candidates. The reason: a significant number of teachers are expected to retire, and there will be the usual turnover among beginning teachers who leave the profession. Even with an expected smaller cohort of students to be educated, the career outlook is positive. Your willingness to relocate to a fast-growing state or region will also increase your chances of securing your first teaching position.

As for higher education and prospective teachers of English, the American Federation of Teachers describes an academic staffing crisis in terms of the availability of tenure-track faculty positions. At the time of publication, only 30 percent of the postsecondary instructional workforce were employed in full-time tenure and tenure-track positions. More than one-third of the workers were part-time/adjunct faculty, 15 percent were full-time non–tenure-track workers, and 20 percent were graduate student employees. Competition for tenure-track positions will be keen given the increasing use of non–tenure-track, part-time/adjunct, and graduate student employees. If you would like to know more about this topic, visit the American Federation of Teachers website (aft.org/topics/academic-staffing).

Strategy for Finding the Jobs: Public Schools

The four tasks outlined—surfing the Web, directly contacting schools where you would like to work, checking with your career office, and scanning relevant newspapers—provide an excellent starting point for your job search.

Surf the Web

Particular websites come and go, but the Internet will always be a good source of job postings for teaching positions. For public school jobs, check out some excellent sites: ed.gov/programs/erod/erodmap.html—simply click on a state to find links to U.S. Education Department–funded organizations that serve that state, including the state's Department of Education. When you drill down, you will find job postings for schools throughout the state. The Academic Employment Network (academploy.com/resources.cfm) also provides access to many, many job listings.

Directly Contact Schools Where You Would Like to Work

Send a cover letter and résumé to schools where you would like to work. State departments of education publish paper and online directories of all public schools in the state, listing superintendents, principals, and principal administrators. Names, addresses, and phone numbers are regularly included in these listings. These same departments of education can provide you with similar information for the state university and technical college systems as well. Many libraries and college career counseling centers will have this same information on file.

Check with Your Career Office

College, university, and technical school career offices in your region of the state will also be on the mailing list to receive teaching vacancy announcements. Determine which schools' jobs postings you can view through reciprocity agreements with your own college and make these visits part of your regular job search. You will find that you become so practiced at screening job postings that it will take very little time to quickly ascertain whether any new openings have been listed.

Scan Relevant Newspapers

The public school teacher candidate is advised to make a regular practice of scanning all newspapers advertising in and around the geographic region being considered for teaching assignments. These newspapers need not be purchased; most libraries subscribe to a generous selection of local papers.

Possible Employers: Public Schools

The *Occupational Outlook Handbook*, 2004–05 edition, published by the U.S. Department of Labor, Bureau of Labor Statistics, reports that 1.1 million of a total of 3.8 million teachers worked as secondary school teachers, and about 10 percent of these people worked for private schools. We often speak of the "hidden job market" in business to refer to the large number of positions that are filled without public notification. But in teaching, in an effort to secure the best pool of applicants as well as to respond to school boards and boards of directors, most positions are well advertised.

Department of Defense (DOD) Schools

Since 1946 there have been schools on U.S. military bases around the world for children of military and civilian personnel assigned overseas. About 220 schools serve this segment of U.S. public education, and courses of study, eligibility for teachers, textbooks, and programs parallel those of the public schools in the United States. Schools in the DOD system are all accredited by appropriate agencies. The program and application processes are outlined in detail on the DOD Education Activity website (dodea.edu).

Strategy for Finding the Jobs: Private Schools

The following two suggestions are critical in helping job seekers find employment in private schools.

Directly Contact Schools Where You Would Like to Work

Send a cover letter and résumé to each private school where you would like to work. Private schools are equally easy to identify through sources such as *Peterson's Guide to Independent Secondary Schools* or the *Handbook of Private Schools* published by Porter Sargent Publishers of Boston. Both of these reference books are standard fare for comprehensive reference sections of career centers and larger college libraries. The National Association of Independent Schools website (nais.org) includes a Career Center. One of the services for job seekers is a list of current job openings.

Attend Job Fairs

Find out about job fairs and attend as many as you can. Job fairs for private schools, both in the United States and abroad, are held year-round. Many are administered by recruiting firms. These fairs serve as an entrée into the private school system for many job seekers. To participate, you register your materials with a private school placement agency, which then provides access to a private school job fair where you can meet and interact with a number of hiring officials from a regional or national base. Your college career office can put you in touch with some of these private school recruiting firms.

Possible Employers: Private Schools

Accessing the private school market is a very different process from seeking a public school situation. In general, there is not a significant amount of crossover between the two systems, and teachers in the private school system tend to spend their careers in that educational environment.

Private schools list positions and send out job notices but seldom advertise in newspapers to ensure a more select pool of candidates and maintain a lower profile than their public counterparts. As tuition-driven institutions, they do not have the core franchise market that public schools automatically obtain and must seek students through reputation and advertising.

Private Schools Abroad

Schools abroad can be researched through directories such as *Schools Abroad of Interest to Americans*, which lists and describes seven hundred elementary and secondary schools in 150 countries that accept English-speaking students. International Schools Services provides services to more than three hundred international schools in some of the remotest locations on the globe. Their publication, the *ISS Directory of International Schools*, identifies this group of potential employers. The International Educator's Institute website (tieonline.com) also contains useful information.

Resources for Finding Both Public and Private School Openings

Educational Directories, a major publisher of educational resources, produces *Patterson's Elementary Education* and *Patterson's American Education* each year.

These publications list public and private elementary and secondary schools, school districts and superintendents, postsecondary schools, and others, including nursery schools, YMCA programs, and the like. Use these directories to conduct your proactive job search activities: mailing out cover letters and résumés, networking, and telephone follow-up.

In addition, review the list of professional associations for teachers of English at the end of this chapter. For several associations there is a line labeled "Job Listings"; any activities that the association undertakes to assist its members in finding employment are shown. The *National Directory for Employment in Education*, a publication of the American Association for Employment in Education (aaee.org), contains a comprehensive registry of professionals at school systems who train, recruit, and hire teachers. Check with your college's education department and career center to find out if they make this publication available to students and alumni.

Strategy for Finding College and University Jobs

Acquiring a college teaching position nearly always demands that you relocate to an institution other than where you received your degree. Higher education has limited openings at any one time, and part-time work or adjunct faculty status at an institution is no guarantee of earning a full-time spot. Most departments have budget lines dedicated to full-time, potentially tenured faculty. This means that faculty who are hired in those budget lines are hired with the expectation they will become a permanent part of the faculty and earn tenure and promotion when they qualify.

Consequently, though there may be schools where you would enjoy teaching or areas of the country you would prefer, the supply and demand of college professorships clearly dictate you must follow the demand and relocate as needed.

Go to "the Source"

The *Chronicle of Higher Education* (chronicle.com) is the weekly national publication listing junior college, four-year college, and university teaching positions in English. Some of these advertisements are large display ads that detail in full the requirements and duties of the positions advertised. This publication is widely available on college campuses, and usually many offices have individual subscriptions. Your career center, department office, and college library will all have copies you can review each week. The website, though, is better than the print version because jobs are clustered on the website by type. In the newspaper edition, you must scan full pages of ads to locate the ones that interest you.

Network with Faculty Colleagues

Another excellent source of college-level positions will be your own faculty colleague contacts made as you pursue your advanced degree. There is a well-established network that becomes very active when schools are seeking to fill a position. This network would value the personal recommendation of a friend or former teaching associate. For this reason, it's important to ensure that your faculty mentors and colleagues are well aware of your teaching and research interests and geographic preferences so they can help move the process along if an opportunity presents itself.

Attend Professional Meetings

Interviews are often conducted at professional meetings, where recent job openings may be announced or posted in a conspicuous place at the registration table. As a graduate student, many of these conferences are available to you at substantially reduced fees or no fee at all. You should take advantage of them for the professional content and the opportunity to meet representatives from the departments of other higher-education institutions.

Possible Employers: Colleges and Universities

Some resources that can be used to identify schools if you are considering teaching English beyond high school include *Peterson's Guide to Two-Year Colleges*, *Peterson's Guide to Four-Year Colleges*, Peterson's annual *Graduate Guide Set* (petersons.com), and the College Board's *Index of Majors and Graduate Degrees*.

Possible Job Titles

For the professional educator, there is not wide latitude in job titles. The term *teacher* is so old and so esteemed that we apply it to professionals from nursery school to the most rarefied levels of postdoctoral research. All are teachers. We see variants from time to time; for example, the resource room teacher in elementary school who works individually with students experiencing difficulties in particular subjects, or the skills application teacher on the college faculty who may have a more narrowly defined teaching role than a staff professor. To students, however, these distinctions may not loom very large, and most are made to indicate bureaucratic distinctions. The teaching role remains the same.

Bilingual teacher
Cooperating teacher
Educator
International school teacher
Resource room teacher
Substitute teacher
Teacher

Related Occupations

Teaching skills and teacher training lend themselves to innumerable occupations and are seen as universally valuable by all other employers.

The ability to explain, demonstrate, encourage, test, and spark imagination can be transferred to countless settings in business and industry. The introduction of new products, cross-training of staff, planning for change or transition, and responding to crises are all situations that call for a teacher's expertise.

Nuclear power information centers, museum programs for children, historical sites, and public relations organizations all have need of the teacher's training in presentation skills, explanation, and the ability to convey meaning.

Social service programs devote much of their mission to education in the form of new programs and information for their clients. This setting uses teachers in situations not very different from the standard classroom. The following list is a brief and general suggestion of possible related careers for the teacher.

Counselor
Education administrator
Educational consultant
Employee development specialist
Employment interviewer
Environmental educator
Hospital/community health educator
Librarian
Media relations representative

Museum curator
Not-for-profit organization administrator
Personnel specialist
Preschool worker
Public relations specialist
Researcher
Sales representative
Social worker
Trainer

Professional Associations for Teachers of English

Finding out about and joining at least one professional association can play an important role in achieving success in your job search. There are many associations that relate to the kinds of jobs available for teachers of English. The following are some groups that can provide valuable information in terms of finding out about actual job listings or talking with members for networking purposes.

American Association for Adult and Continuing Education
4380 Forbes Blvd.
Lanham, MD 20746
aaace.org
Members/Purpose: Provides leadership in advancing education as a lifelong learning process; serves as a central forum for a wide variety of adult and continuing education special-interest groups
Training: Sponsors conferences and meetings
Journals/Publications: *AAACE Online*, *Adult Education Quarterly*, *Adult Learning*

American Association of Community Colleges
One Dupont Circle NW, Suite 410
Washington, DC 20036-1176
aacc.nche.edu
Members/Purpose: Administrators, students, trustees, faculty, public officials, and interested individuals from all segments of postsecondary education; seeks to clarify and help resolve critical issues in postsecondary education through conferences, publications, and special projects

Training: Hosts annual convention
Journals/Publications: *Community College Journal, Community College Times*
Job Listings: Website contains a Career Center Job Bank.

American Association of State Colleges and Universities
1307 New York Ave. NW
Washington, DC 20005-4701
aascu.org
Members/Purpose: Colleges and universities offering programs leading to a degree of bachelor, master, or doctor that are wholly or partially state supported and controlled
Training: Hosts annual meeting and various conferences
Journal/Publication: Biweekly e-newsletter

American Association of University Professors
1012 14th St. NW, Suite 500
Washington, DC 20005
aaup.org
Members/Purpose: College and university teachers, research scholars, and academic librarians; purposes are to advance academic freedom and shared governance, to define fundamental professional values and standards for higher education, and to ensure higher education's contribution to the common good
Journal/Publication: *Academe* bimonthly magazine

American Council on Education
One Dupont Circle NW, Suite 800
Washington, DC 20036
acenet.edu
Members/Purpose: A council of colleges and universities, educational organizations, and affiliates
Journal/Publication: *The Presidency* magazine

American Federation of Teachers
555 New Jersey Ave. NW
Washington, DC 20001
aft.org
Members/Purpose: Represents the economic, social, and professional interests of classroom teachers; an affiliated international union of the AFL-CIO

Journals/Publications: *American Educator, American Teacher, Healthwire, AFT on Campus, PSRP Reporter, Public Employee Advocate, American Academic*

American Society for Training and Development
1640 King St., Box 1443
Alexandria, VA 22313
astd.org
Members/Purpose: Professional association for persons engaged in training and development for business, industry, education, and government; undertakes special research projects and acts as a clearinghouse
Training: Hosts conferences
Journal/Publication: *T&D Magazine*
Job Listings: Online careers job bank lists available positions

Council for American Private Education
13017 Wisteria Dr., Suite 457
Germantown, MD 20874
capenet.org
Members/Purpose: Coalition of national organizations serving the interests of private schools (K–12)
Journal/Publication: *Outlook* newsletter
Job Listings: Online links to private school job banks

Modern Language Association
26 Broadway, 3rd floor
New York, NY 10004-1789
mla.org
Members/Purpose: Promotes the study and teaching of language and literature
Training: Hosts annual convention
Journal/Publication: *MLA Newsletter*
Job Listings: Online job information list

National Association of Independent Schools
1620 L St. NW, 11th Floor
Washington, DC 20036
nais-schools.org
Members/Purpose: Independent elementary and secondary school members; regional associations of independent schools and related associations; provides curricular and administrative research and services

Training: Conducts seminars
Journals/Publications: *Independent School, NAIS e-Bulletin*
Job Listings: Online career center includes job listings

National Council of Teachers of English
1111 Kenyon Rd.
Urbana, IL 61801
ncte.org
Members/Purpose: Teachers of English at all school levels; works to
   increase the effectiveness of instruction in English language and
   literature
Training: Hosts workshops, institutes, and conventions
Journals/Publications: *Language Arts, School Talk, Voices from the Middle*

National Educational Association
1201 16th St. NW
Washington, DC 20036
nea.org
Members/Purpose: Professional organization and union of elementary and
   secondary school teachers, college and university professors,
   administrators, principals, counselors, and others concerned with
   education
Journals/Publications: *NEA Today, This Active Life* magazine, *Tomorrow's
   Teachers* magazine, *Higher Education Advocate*

Path 3:
Advertising and
Public Relations

An attractive mystique surrounds the fields of advertising and public relations, and not only for the English major. These fields are seen, and justifiably so in most instances, as glamorous, high-visibility industries. Not only are advertising and public relations omnipresent in today's society, but we are also fascinated with the mechanics of how they are accomplished and what works and what doesn't. Advertising campaigns become the subject of morning-after conferences in the workplace, and the latest spokesperson's financial deal is the subject of newspaper headlines. Working in these fields seems to convey to the employee a halo of quickness, creativity, and imagination—not all of which may be warranted. We associate advertising with celebrity, which may or may not be justified. Advertising is not only omnipresent in society; it can be (and has been) the subject of great controversy, subsequently attracting enormous press coverage in and of itself.

Advertising continues to be a medium of social change in the United States. Increasingly, ads are targeted at very specific audiences. The music, setting, and choice of actors all combine to create a message directed at a very specific group of the buying public. With so many advertising messages constantly being aired, individual advertisers will frequently "push the envelope" of taste and/or discretion to have their product noticed in hopes the public will be provoked to some kind of reaction.

Public relations has also come into the common vocabulary as we become more aware of how organizations, products, and personalities manage their public presence in our lives. One example that emphasizes the importance of public relations to the viability of a company was Merck and Company's response to the first Vioxx trial in which a jury awarded $253 million to the widow of a man who died after taking the painkiller Vioxx for several months. In a news release, the senior VP and general counsel of Merck described how the company had acted responsibly by researching the product prior to approval, by monitoring the medicine while it was on the market, and by voluntarily withdrawing the medicine from the marketplace. As trials continue, the company's skillful handling of public relations during this crisis will be critical to the solvency of this global pharmaceutical company.

Much is written and broadcast about the behind-the-scenes work of both public relations and advertising managers. Not all of it is positive, and occasionally we see instances of downright duplicity, but both fields remain centers of creativity, originality, and impact. Because of that, they justify being called glamour jobs.

Getting the Message Across

For the English major interested in a graphic illustration of the shifting importance of language in both public relations and advertising, a fascinating comparison would be to look at advertising from the 1950s and advertising from the present. You'll notice in the older advertisements a far greater reliance on textual material. People read ads, and there was a significant amount of straightforward text. Today, people view ads and respond far more to color and photographic images than to factual detail. Our increasing fascination with photographs means they are used far more often than the printed word to convey meaning. Today, we only see text-heavy copy in advertisements for very costly or highly complex products. Generally, commercial advertising has become a visual medium, and product presentation through the use of words has taken second place to art, atmosphere, and personalities.

Public relations has also undergone a revolution over the past few decades. In the 1950s, public relations may have simply meant responding to a consumer's letter of compliment or complaint and answering inquiries about product composition or manufacturing processes. American society was enjoying a booming proliferation of consumer goods, variations on product themes, and even packaging. This was a far cry from our concerns today, where much of such proliferation is being rejected or subjected to intense scrutiny. But during the '50s, the public was largely an adulatory audience to the manufacturer and wanted more, not less.

Today public relations departments have many more interested observers and critics carefully watching the organization's performance from the vantage point of whatever special-interest group they represent: environmental, nutritional, child protective rights, gender equity issues, product quality, or full-disclosure concerns. These groups recognize the impact corporations can have on our quality of life and the influence they can exert on public opinion, social structure, moral issues, and values. Many argue that just the prevalence of corporate messages sends a disturbing signal about acquisitiveness and self-indulgence. More than ever before, a business must be prepared to answer to numerous publics on equally as many issues.

Some organizations have learned a difficult lesson from not having a crisis management team to deal with threats from the outside that might have permanent negative effects on the organization's product, image, or continued existence. Now, corporations frequently have departments or at least teams who handle crisis management. These personnel are trained to provide information to the public about the crisis, organize and manage product recall if necessary, and create mechanisms to prevent reoccurrence if possible.

Public relations has become increasingly complex, the situations are often serious, and the concerns of the public are legitimate and insistent. Public relations must become increasingly proactive; therefore, the field is more in need of good writers and communicators than ever before. Both advertising and public relations still welcome the English major who is interested in the field of persuasive communications. A number of avenues are possible in both fields, and both offer much creativity and opportunity to touch the lives of people in meaningful and unexpected ways.

Definition of the Career Path

Public relations and advertising are often linked, but in fact they are two very different fields of public communication with different aims, techniques, and intentions. Nevertheless, we usually refer to them in one phrase, and with good reason. Most firms that buy advertising and use it to promote their corporate image, products, or ideas will probably at some time need public relations to explain, clarify, or deal with sectors of the public that take issue with the organization over some aspect of its operation.

Public Relations

Public relations is that function of an organization that seeks to maintain good relations with any number of publics it must interact with in doing business. A good example may be the popular American fast-food chain McDonald's. The publics McDonald's must stay responsive to are many. They include environmentalists who are concerned about such issues as packaging. Or city and town planners who worry about issues such as signage and sign height, curb cuts to allow entrance and exit to parking lots, and the physical impact of a restaurant on their municipality. And there are school officials who may be concerned that the restaurant might become a hangout or who fear many children will work excessive part-time hours and diminish their school performance. Another public includes zoning officials who worry about spot-rezoning planned neighborhoods to accommodate a McDonald's restaurant. One more group is made up of nutritionists who want consumers to understand the caloric, sodium, and fat content and nutritional composition of products. The list could go on and on.

Each of these groups has issues over this internationally famous restaurant chain's operation. Public relations officials seek not only to understand the points of view of these groups, but also to have these groups understand McDonald's point of view on the concerns they may hold particularly important. The award-winning documentary *Supersize Me*, by Morgan Spurlock, looked at the legal, financial, and physical costs of America's hunger for fast food and specifically targeted McDonald's. The film spurred an outcry from many health-oriented individuals and organizations and led to McDonald's launch of a new worldwide initiative in early 2005 that promoted healthy living in an effort to combat criticism of its food and business. Public relations professionals played a key role in explaining the introduction of new products and the healthiness of existing products in efforts to sway the critics.

Who Is the Public? You may have noticed that customers were not in the list of publics. Customers are not part of the public in the term *public relations*. Customers are the focus of advertising, marketing, operations, and product delivery. The customer is the "business" that a firm is about. Certain publics may take issue with the organization as it does business with the market, and public relations is the arm of an institution that takes responsibility for dealing with these noncustomer publics. The public relations department may respond to individual consumer concerns by providing needed technical data, but as a group, consumers are categorized separately.

It isn't just commercial enterprises that have need of public relations. Public relations exists in any large institution; even colleges and universities have need of public relations. Perhaps neighbors are upset over streets jammed with cars every time there's a football game on Saturday at a major university, or about shifting property values as students take over nearby dwellings for apartment buildings. Public relations officers handle these situations and help the parties reach solutions. They also draw the public's attention to efforts undertaken by the institution, for example, the new city park built and financed through student efforts or the care for elders provided by a fraternity or sorority house. No public relations staff member expects all assignments to be positive ones, but part of the job is to ensure that the public has the full picture of an organization.

Our McDonald's example hardly exhausted the range of publics that a public relations department deals with, however. Other aspects of public relations include public information provided to concerned groups and individuals to explain changes in operations, product quality information, or initiatives undertaken by the corporation. This may seem relatively static, but part of good public relations is being able to document this kind of consistent public disclosure to prevent accusations of conspiracy or undue secrecy. Most firms issue regular press releases that announce expansion plans, new factory sites, potential layoffs, new products, product recalls, and a host of other events of at least some interest to the public.

Communicating the Message. Whenever a corporation makes information public by press release; newsletter; a mass mailing to customers, clients, or investors; television announcement; or major newspaper display ad, the public relations knows best how to present the message of the organization to the public at large. Mobil Corporation, which has certainly had ample opportunity to test the merits of its corporate communications department, pioneered the *advertorial*, a paid piece of advertising designed and written to resemble an editorial piece. These are thoughtful and thought-provoking pieces of writing to keep the public thinking about the role of oil energy and the impact of that product in our lives. Today organizations have the option to create these messages internally or to outsource this work. If you use your favorite search engine and enter the word *advertorial*, you will see how important these communications have become given the hundreds of thousands of hits you'll get.

Keeping Investors Informed. Investor relations is a public relations function organized to meet the needs of individuals who have invested in the organization through stock purchases or other mechanisms and who tend to be among the most vocal and active of publics. These members have a right and obligation as investors to thoroughly understand company operations and policy. Public relations produces informative material to keep these investors abreast of profits, losses, future plans, personnel, and the financial stability of the firm.

Addressing Questions from Customers. Consumer services is yet another public relations division that answers customers' questions about product handling, quality, manufacturing processes, safety, and even student requests for company information to do research reports. In fact, some organizations provide quite extensive consumer services, and most now maintain websites and toll-free numbers. As with all public relations efforts, the purpose is twofold. In satisfying consumer requests for information and by being accessible, the company increases the probability of a positive relationship with both customers and the general public and assures its continued presence in the marketplace.

The Importance of Research. A research department of a large public relations division might support public relations by providing the necessary factual data to most accurately and honestly respond to a variety of situations. Researchers can ascertain how much of a product is sold, where in the world certain raw materials used in the manufacturing process are obtained, the origin of the labor pool, the origin of specific parts used in making the product, and any other information required by the public relations department. A consumer may, for example, ask about a chemical or ingredient to which he or she is sensitive that is not listed on the packaging of a particular product but may be used in processing or in other products made on the same equipment and thus could potentially lead to an allergic reaction and perhaps serious health consequences. If the public relations department does not immediately know the answer to such a query, it could direct the problem to the organization's research arm.

A Focus on Internal Constituents. Employees staff the organization, but they are also a public that needs to understand the corporation's mission because they serve as the corporation's ambassadors in their personal lives. Likewise, employees need to be understood by management so that an effective team is formed and sustained as products or services are produced and delivered to the consumer. Corporate newsletters, picnics, interest-free Christmas loans, or on-site child care or elder care are all projects in which public relations team members might participate. You might have seen television commercials showing various employees in an organization going about their jobs. General Motors and other automobile manufacturers have been notable in this regard. Such commercials certainly put an individual face on a large corporation for average consumers, but they also serve to instill pride and loyalty in the workforce that is being featured.

Sample Job Postings. The following advertisements are actual job postings for public relations staffers that would be particularly attractive to a college English major. See what they can tell you about the job and the organization:

Internal Communications Specialist. Manufacturing company. Assist with the development and implementation of internal communications strategies using a variety of print, video, and electronic media. The specialist will also serve as editor of a weekly company-wide newsletter. Requires outstanding writing, editing, and communications skills; good organizational skills; outstanding team focus; bachelor's degree in communications or a related field.

Public Relations Specialist. Communications and brand consulting firm. Responsibilities include interviewing agency contacts to develop story angles and write news releases to generate publicity; coordinating all aspects of support materials for media pitches, including photography and other visual elements; interfacing with media contacts in a backup capacity; researching and maintaining media contacts database; pitching stories as assigned; writing and maintaining agency bios. Bachelor's degree required, prefer some background in public relations, and strong writing skills.

Media/Public Relations Assistant. Fast-paced ad agency looking for an organized, outgoing, and dependable individual able to work in a team environment. Must be detail oriented, possess strong grammatical and communications skills, and be a self-starter who takes initiative. Must be proficient in Microsoft Office with emphasis on Word and Excel. Bachelor's degree in communications, journalism, or English.

Advertising

Advertising is the world of paid persuasive communications that reach consumers through the mass media. The design, production, and execution of an advertisement for a website, magazine, newspaper, or TV or radio spot must accomplish several things. Advertisements are intended to remind customers of a product, to highlight a need for that product, to inform the audience of a product's availability and the identity and location of the seller, or to detail product features and compare them to the competition. Advertisers like to create excitement around their products by developing an image and identity that will clearly separate the product from that of the competition.

As products and their uses change over time, advertisers often need to create advertising to demonstrate to the public new ways of thinking about and using their products. The classic example of such repositioning might be the condom. For most of its product history, the condom was used to prevent pregnancy. However, with the arrival of AIDS, condom use began to be advocated as a method of disease prevention and condom manufacturers responded with advertising that featured this product advantage.

Before You See the Ad. Before ads reach the public, much activity has already taken place. Most of the planning for advertising is done with written communications that outline ideas, document various proposals, and suggest possible themes. Ultimately this written work culminates in formal presentation documents that put forth a commercial idea and its associated costs before the officials who provide the goods or services being advertised and who will fund the cost of the advertising.

Account executives will present numerous ideas and rationales on paper to company agents suggesting possible advertising campaign themes, such as scripts for TV advertising, radio spots, in-theater commercials, telemarketing activities, and print advertising. This is the work of the copywriter. Although the copywriter's work is the most obvious and creative use of words seen by the commercial consumer, there is much behind that work. Efforts include building an advertising concept, creating a unique selling proposition to the public that will help to separate this product from its peers, developing the rationale for the ad, and preparing ideas, proposals, and presentations to advertising agencies, artists, and owner representatives.

Using the Language of the Marketplace. Ad agencies are built on words. Advertising people care deeply about words, enjoy them, and value people who can use them effectively and even dramatically. But they are not sticklers about correct language; they listen to the language of the market they hope to speak to. They mimic the vocabulary, syntax, and phrases of that market. When the market sees or hears this work, consumers should think, "They're talking to me!" That is when the writer has been successful.

Enhancing the Product's Impact. Advertising departments include creative services, which can realize packaging, logotypes, design concepts, slogans, signature lines, and any kind of concept or visual to enhance the impact of the product that appears before the public. Although much of this work may be subcontracted to smaller "boutique" type agencies, especially in cases of music services or voice-overs, creative control is exercised by the agency and the account executives managing that particular client's account.

These account executives have helped to develop the concept and will ensure that any participating services, performers, designers, and copywriters who become involved maintain a fidelity to the original concept. The integrity of this concept and the adjusting of advertising to match it are the subject of countless memoranda, letters, and notes exchanged between account executives and the providers of individual services, who may be at some distance from the original concept.

Timing the Message. Media services is a common area of entry into an agency and involves the scheduling and buying of media time for an account. How commercial messages are timed for frequency in any particular time period (month, season, year) can have a tremendous impact on the public's response. The buying of media is a sophisticated art blending knowledge of the market, understanding the best media approach to that market, and knowing the optimum listening or viewing times, repetition frequency, and length and content of the message for the market. If there is too little exposure the impact will be weak; if there is too much there actually may be a negative reaction to the product. Each additional dollar spent on media should ideally add customers. Media buying requires creativity to work effectively.

Perhaps you are promoting a movie about a mother and daughter, both parts being played by actresses popular with their own age groups. Running a movie commercial featuring the mother during daytime or late afternoon talk-show time slots (a time period favored by mature women) and a different commercial featuring the younger actress during prime-time situation comedy slots would attract both audience segments.

Managing Clients' Needs: Account Executives. The senior account executives who manage individual client accounts are drawn from across all agency departments and have the experience to manage general oversight of a client's total advertising effort with the agency. They schedule and conduct meetings and presentations for the client, interact with subcontractors, manage billing, and, most important, work with the client to achieve the most distinctive campaign or advertisement possible for the medium and cost. These individuals are excellent communicators, both verbally and on paper. Many an advertising executive is also a short-story writer, novelist, poet, playwright, or screenwriter. Legions of published writers have been incubated in advertising agencies.

Advertising account executive is an exciting, fast-paced career position with frequent changes of jobs between agencies as executives seek new arenas to exercise their talents. Clients also frequently change agencies, even when their current agency does superior work. After lengthy association with an agency, clients may simply wonder if someone else couldn't "spark" their advertising efforts in a unique way. This kind of movement of both executives and clients suggests the need for a high tolerance of risk and low need for job security.

Ad Agency or In-House? Not all advertising is done in a professional advertising agency. Many organizations have their own advertising departments, which replicate in many aspects the functions of a full-fledged agency. Often these in-house agencies will do everything up until the actual purchase of print or broadcast media time.

Brand Management. Consumer goods firms also have individuals charged with brand management. These executives have the responsibility for all activities surrounding a particular branded product, such as Minute Maid orange juice, Scotch tape dispensers, or Hellmann's mayonnaise. They manage all aspects of production, product sizing, sales promotion, and advertising. They exercise a strong influence on advertising initiatives for their product line and work closely with in-house and contracted outside agencies to produce effective advertising for their product.

Sample Job Postings. Here are some recent entry-level job postings in the field of advertising:

Assistant Brand Manager. Assist with new package design development; execution and collation of SKU data; new product development; identifying new product opportunities; researching current dynamics in the marketplace; writing design briefs; verbally briefing design agency; managing iterative design process; developing coupons. Requires four-year degree, strong verbal and written ability to communicate, strategic thinking, analytical approach to problem solving, attention to detail, and organizational skills.

Copywriter. Responsible for planning, managing, and maintaining compelling marketing materials and information resources in support of our sales and marketing goals. Requires a four-year degree and some copywriting experience.

Marketing Coordinator. Responsibilities include market research, development and implementation of marketing programs, event planning, and working on special projects. Requires bachelor's degree in business, journalism, or related field; ability to work under pressure in a fast-paced environment; and excellent communications and time management skills.

Public Relations and Advertising: The Common Denominators

We have made a distinction between the fields of advertising and public relations, but the question remains, why group them together if they are, in fact, so different? It's a reasonable question with a logical answer. Both advertising and public relations have a message to convey to the public. To do that most effectively requires an understanding of who the public is, how members of the target market think, and what language, images, ideas, and words they are most likely to respond to.

Using the Power of Persuasion. Another shared dimension of the communications of both advertising and public relations is that they are persuasive in tone. Advertising seeks to move the market to excitement, change of attitude, and ultimately purchase. The public relations approach may be more subtle, but it also seeks to influence public thinking and behavior about an organization. Public relations communications seek to persuade the public to perceive the organization in a certain way; to understand its position, mission, and goals; and to appreciate its contribution to our life and society in general.

Building Broad Awareness and Appreciation. In both fields the precise word, tone, and nuance of the message can have significant reverberations for the organization or product being represented. These fields both require not only a masterful grasp of English, but also a real sense of the sweep of the English language, both historically and in its most recent incarnations. Along with these language skills must come a very high level of general information. Advertisers need to know at least something about almost everything, and public relations people have to be equally in tune with their audience. For example, if a public relations department sends out correspondence regarding environmental issues, sending that message on recycled paper (labeled as such) and printed with environmentally approved soy-based ink would be noticed and appreciated by the audience and would help to condition the audience's response to the message.

Effective messages are based on such connections with the audience. So it isn't enough to know about sports and athletes if your next client is a music producer representing a violin virtuoso. Pest exterminators, AIDS activists, microchip manufacturers, department stores, insurance companies, and thousands of other organizations seek advertising and public relations assistance. A limitation in terms of awareness of and appreciation for the clients' products and services could be your biggest liability.

Using Technology. The need for computer skills, especially desktop publishing and graphics familiarity, is particularly acute in both advertising and public relations. If you are contemplating either of these careers and are still in college, take advantage of your computer science or graphic arts department course offerings and build some expertise in this area to add to your desirability as a job candidate.

Developing a Deep-Rooted Understanding. Personal characteristics of advertising executives have tended to overstress the need for creativity. Certainly there is a demand for quickness, the ability to generate ideas, and the ability to be intuitive about a product and how best to present that product. But most advertising professionals will say that their best efforts are actually born from a deep understanding of the product and marketplace. The concepts and appeals they create develop quite organically from their research on the market and the product. Advertising has become a highly quantitative business; people spending money on advertising expect some reasonable quantification of return on their investment. How many people will see a particular print ad or view a commercial? What percentage of sales increase might be realized in a geographic market as the result of special advertising programs? What would be the net effect of in-store promotions versus broadcast media for a product?

For those in public relations, personal characteristics would include a sense of poise even under pressure and a good sense of humor, even of the absurd! The ability to remain cool and collected in stressful situations is important to ensure that any communications you give out in times of stress (crisis management, unusual incidents, natural disasters) are statements you can live with long after the incident. Diplomacy, thoughtfulness, and a real sensitivity to the concerns of interested publics are also important. If you are helping to stage a reception for distinguished foreign guests, should you serve cuisine of their country, American food, or perhaps some combination? What would suit the audience and the situation? Public relations professionals are masters of anticipation. They are constantly thinking of how any action, statement, or initiative on the part of their organization may be perceived or misperceived by the public.

Adding to the Team. Much of both advertising and public relations is teamwork, so the ability to work in groups is quite important to success. It is difficult to generalize about other desired characteristics in the successful advertising executive and public relations official. Both have room for a great many personalities with as many skills and talents. Both will tolerate an extreme range of personalities if the person can produce effective work. Most effective workers in this area, however, probably are curious about people's behavior and values and the marketplace itself. Many are widely read and enjoy staying current with literature, art, music, the theater, and athletics. They are intensely aware of social and political events and how these can affect the public's collective consciousness. They are often predictors of trends and fads.

Helping to Move the Cause Forward. Careers develop in advertising and public relations in a somewhat similar fashion. Advertising careers are made by how well you do for a particular account. This means not only how much your advertising is noticed, but also how effectively it moves consumers to do what you hoped they would, which might be simply to remember the product's name. Public relations success is accelerated when you are helpful in responding to a difficult situation for an organization or managing a successful change in image or a repositioning of the organization in the public's mind.

Competing for the Job. Entry into either advertising or public relations can be discouraging because, as with so many "glamour" jobs, most of the glamour is misunderstood. The lines of applicants are long, however, and competition is stiff. Some kind of related experience would be helpful. Meeting practitioners and learning about their experiences and views of the business would also be of immense value. For advertising, it may be best to think not in terms of a job in advertising, but a job in one of the media, for example, radio, TV, or print. Build your expertise in a department such as scheduling or sales and then bring that experience to an advertising agency.

Public relations has its own grooming process. To speak with authority and credibility for the organization, you need significant experience at a senior level to know what to say and how to say it. It is not uncommon for senior public relations officials to have been leaders of a number of different divisions. It is through long experience that the trust an organization must place in its spokesperson is born. He or she has earned this trust over time and in many roles.

Because advertising is predominant in American society, many organizations have done very well through their advertising efforts, and even small organizations have taken it upon themselves to buy advertising services. Public relations has also grown as an industry, although as a specialty it has not achieved the stature of advertising because a firm needs to reach a certain size in terms of output, staff, and impact to feel the need to respond to its publics in a formal, planned manner. Likewise, the public doesn't always demand a professional level of response from a smaller firm. Consequently, you will find fewer public relations opportunities with small firms than are found in advertising.

Advancing in Your Career. Often practitioners of both public relations and advertising see career growth by moving to larger and larger clients and increasing the size of their staffs and budgets in the process. Issues and challenges become correspondingly larger, and the opportunity for great success or public failure is an element of risk. Even the most skilled advertisers with extensive staffs and budgets can produce advertisements that not only don't do what they set out to accomplish, but might, in fact, attract negative publicity. Likewise, skilled public relations professionals can misjudge the significance of a situation and fail to exercise judicious damage control at the proper time, letting a difficult situation go from bad to worse. It is just this risk—the potential for failure or success—that many in advertising and public relations find exciting. These fields are highly dependent on the professional's "reading" of the public's attitudes and disposition toward the organization or product.

Enjoying the Rewards. What are the rewards of working in public relations or advertising? Both involve teamwork; consequently, those who enjoy working with other individuals and the camaraderie and esprit de corps that develop will enjoy this aspect of the work. Using your intelligence, creativity, understanding of the public, intuition, artistic sense, critical judgment, and analytical ability can allow you to feel an exciting sense of "stretch" and personal development. Both fields test the individual's skills and attributes. If you enjoy that kind of testing in a work environment, you will find advertising and public relations stimulating and challenging.

Working Conditions

The similarities and differences between advertising and public relations working conditions are described here.

Advertising

Advertising working conditions are centered on the product and the market for the product. Advertising professionals need to be aware of the news and social trends, for in any of these events may come an indication of change that may impact how a product should be presented or how a product's reception may change. Aspirin, for example, was originally used to relieve pain. Now, producers of aspirin are touting it as a wonder drug. Some researchers believe it may reduce the risk of colorectal cancer, and most manufacturers encourage aspirin regimens to reduce the risk of heart attack. There is aspirin plus calcium for women, chewable aspirin for children, aspirin cream for muscle and joint pain, aspirin for rapid headache relief, and low-dose safety coated aspirin, just to name a few.

So advertisers must stay current on social thinking and trends. Consequently, advertising offices and departments are social centers with much collaboration and shared idea generation. Everything is grist for the advertising mill. Much planning goes into advertising, but new ideas are welcome and risks are often taken in the hopes of increasing market share for a product. For established products of stable demand, advertisers simply try to create the most effective distribution of their message through the appropriate media for the budget they have been allotted.

Advertising offices exhibit all kinds of energy levels, from frantic activity to intense concentration, depending on what stage of the process or what kind of account the workers are focusing on at the time. They are fast-paced, active, "let's do it" climates with high energy levels that require a high tolerance for stress.

Public Relations

Public relations offers two different working conditions. For most public relations, there is significant ordered planning to build and achieve rapport with any number of publics. Many situations require research, careful thought, and solid preparation to ensure that the organization's goals and mission are presented accurately and that material is available to meet the questions and concerns of interested publics. Some of these situations include formal presentations, responses to letters or complaints, court cases, consumer disputes, company expansion plans, or new product launches.

This proactive work may involve placing informative messages in major media publications, direct mailings to customers or investors, telemarketing, press conferences, or press kits to the media. In most instances, public relations are ongoing, although there may be short-term goals for a particular reason, for example price hikes or a product recall.

Sometimes, however, plans don't go as intended. Accidents occur, violence takes place, nature intervenes, production lines fail, or any of a million possible negative situations occurs. Then the public relations department is called in to respond and set things right: alert the public to alternative product sources, describe how to file a reimbursement claim, or explain how to return a damaged product. Some of these situations could be classified as crisis management. Most public relations experts will tell you that although you cannot anticipate a crisis, you can plan for it by suggesting certain scenarios and determining in advance what might be the best response for the organization in such an eventuality. The more alternatives and situations you can anticipate, the faster and more effectively you can respond when an event occurs.

Even though you may have planned for a particular crisis, it is still a time of stress if it actually develops. For the duration of the problem, the public relations department may find itself the press headquarters of an organization—granting interviews, writing news stories, providing press releases, all of which must be carefully considered to maintain public confidence in the product or service and the organization.

Training and Qualifications

A review of some of the actual advertisements for entry-level positions in advertising and public relations will clearly demonstrate that with your English degree you have the basic qualifications for work in these fields. If you are a skillful user of English both verbally and in written formats, you'll be very competitive. Add some computer familiarity (word processing at least; desktop publishing is a plus), and you'll find you fit the bill for most entry-level positions.

This is good news for English majors. However, there is a caution attached! The basic skills and a little more may get your foot in the proverbial door, but from that point on, the qualifications become less specific and more difficult to pin down.

Both areas demand a high level of general information. Because these fields are essentially barometers of social trends, the qualified candidate needs to be a highly aware individual. You cannot afford to ignore certain fields of human activity. For example, perhaps you find professional wrestling childish, contrived, and repellent, so you have always ignored it and its personalities. However, as an advertising executive, you may be managing the promotion events for a line of toys or clothing or board games based on this sport. In public relations, you may need to secure the services of a currently popular wrestler to promote your company's or client's product.

The people who populate the fields of advertising and public relations are marked by their diversity, their wide range of interests, and their encyclopedic knowledge of current events, human activity, politics, and personalities. They can talk on the latest medical developments in the search for a cure for cystic fibrosis and move on to experimental opera. They are, and you should be, too, inveterate readers. They watch television and go to films, theater, car rallies, rodeos, concerts, and other types of events.

To communicate effectively with the public, you need to understand all kinds of human activities, not just those that you personally prefer. You will need to appreciate varying public tastes, needs, wants, and desires and how they are expressed in order to effectively communicate through the medium of advertising or public relations.

A valuable test of your own preparedness for these fields as well as a qualifying training experience in and of itself is the internship. This will be an education in what professionals do in these fields as well as a close-up observation of the personalities that inhabit them. You'll learn some skills, practice many others, and take stock of how well you measure up to expectations and norms.

Most important, given the intense and unrelenting competitive demand for positions in these fields, the internship provides yet another notch in your handle of experience. Examine some of the excellent internship directories, such as the American Advertising Federation's *Internship Directory* (aaf.org/college/internships.html), *National Directory of Arts Internships* (artistplacement.com), and *Peterson's Internships* (http://testnas.petersons.com/books). They list hundreds of organizations from coast to coast offering public relations and advertising internships in museums, social service agencies, theaters, festivals, university settings, environmental organizations, women's centers, juvenile courts, TV and radio stations, and zoos. Look for these directories in your career-office library or public library. You will find internships listed on the Internet as well. Simply use your favorite search engine and start looking!

Earnings

Salaries for established professionals are usually based on the span of control, budgetary authority, and educational and experiential background. When entry-level positions are examined, factors affecting salary include size, geographic location, billing size, and type of organization.

Advertising

The Internet can be a useful resource for finding the latest earnings information for jobs in the advertising industry. Career websites such as career mosaic.com and commercial sites such as Advertising Age's site (adage.com) provide lots of useful information, including some salaries. Keep in mind that salaries will vary by type of agency, billing size, and region of the country. At the time of this writing, the following entry-level salaries were available for those working in either an agency or for a corporation:

- Media buyer: $40,750
- Media planner: $42,000
- Advertising coordinator: $38,900
- Marketing assistant: $35,300–$40,000

Public Relations

PR Week regularly publishes salary surveys, and it reports average entry-level salary information for the industry. The 2005 salary survey listed an entry-level salary range of $36,331 to $37,038. At the time of printing, Wageweb (wageweb.com), an online salary service, lists average minimum salaries for a public relations representative as $31,322. Be sure to check the latest information available on both websites.

Career Outlook

For those seeking entry-level positions in public relations, the competition will be keen. As we discussed, many new college graduates are interested in working in this field, and the number of job openings is often smaller than the number of qualified applicants. Related summer work and internships along with relevant course work will positively affect your standing in the applicant pool. Be sure to review the section entitled "Strategy for Finding the Jobs" for additional suggestions.

Advertising-industry employment is expected to grow steadily through the year 2012, according to the *Occupational Outlook Handbook*. Factors affecting advertising employment include both domestic and global competition in products and services. As consumers draw from both domestic and international markets, there will be a corresponding demand on advertisers and marketers to master the promotional, communications, and advertising strategies needed to succeed in this evolving business environment.

Strategy for Finding the Jobs

The four tasks outlined here create a comprehensive strategy for finding work in advertising and public relations.

Highlight Relevant Course Work

Employers want to know about relevant courses you've taken—they will serve as part of the foundation that will make you a valued and productive employee. For advertising positions some relevant course work includes marketing, consumer behavior, market research, sales, communication methods and technology, and visual arts (art history, photography, and so on). In public relations, the following courses are beneficial: advertising, business administration, public affairs, public speaking, political science, and creative and technical writing.

Because you will be presenting your degree in English, rather than a business degree, as your educational credential, it is especially important to highlight relevant courses. Some of these classes, for example, communication methods, creative writing, and technical writing, may have been part of your degree program. You may have taken other courses as part of a minor or to meet a general education requirement. Be sure to put this relevant coursework on your résumé and talk about it during the interview. You will also need to express your interest in participating in professional development opportunities that will bring you up to speed in other areas.

Review Job Advertisements

Read job listings on the Internet and in the papers—they will help you learn job titles, duties, and responsibilities for various jobs and get some sense of salary levels. Determine which job advertisements mesh with your interests and background and then how you can refine your résumé and cover letter. It is important to know what's out there, both the good and the not so good.

Hit the Streets!

Most job listings in advertising and public relations that you come across will be for specialized experience (which you do not yet have) or will be low-level clerical/administrative jobs that you would not enjoy and, more important, would not learn from. The wisdom on the street for jobs in these fields is that it is best to directly contact an agency or organization for which you want to work. The best cover letter and résumé in advertising and public relations is the one that's hand delivered. The supply of candidates in advertising and public relations so far outweighs demand for available positions that job-seekers must literally go straight to the employers. This standard is so developed that employers ignore résumés that arrive by mail. With job candidates walking in the door, employers don't need to answer letters that suggest they call the job seeker if interested.

Keep Checking with Potential Employers

If an agency principal is looking to fill a position, chances are he or she doesn't have to do much more than wander out to the office lobby and see who is at the reception desk trying desperately to see someone about a job. There is a logic here, as well. The kind of assertiveness, persistence, and "go-for-it" drive that would bring an individual to the agency in person are just the qualities that are called for in advertising and public relations. If you want to get a job, yours will be the face that the receptionist sees on a fairly regular basis.

Possible Employers

There is a range of possible employers for those interested in working in advertising or public relations. The list includes advertising agencies, TV stations, radio stations, specialty advertisers, outdoor advertising agencies, magazines, newspapers, public relations firms, utilities, sports organizations, the U.S. government, state and local governments, educational institutions, medical institutions, and associations. Let's review a series of possible employer types with an accent on the English major. Because many employer directories and job listings sources cover all or many of these employer types, we'll provide a basic library of listings and resources to locate these employers. Give each type of employer your full consideration and begin your job search by contacting the type of employer you are most interested in working with.

Advertising Agencies

Advertising agencies continue to break new ground in communicating with the public, despite the continuing proliferation of products and "noise" surrounding each of those products. Although advertisements have become increasingly visual, writers are still needed for copy used in print ads, voiceovers in films and videos, and product packaging. Even in the purest visual advertisement, the effectiveness is achieved because behind and supporting the ad is a position paper outlining the intent, scope, and focus of the proposed piece of advertising. Communication remains the mainstay of the independent advertising agency. The demand is still crucial for strong and creative communication that will arrest the public's attention and move people to some desired response.

TV Stations

TV stations are supported by the advertising that is placed with them. Advertising departments for TV stations work to attract and hold potential advertisers by offering them time and day slots for their advertising that will best deliver the correct market for the advertiser's product. Because of these stations' technical capabilities, they are frequently called on to produce commercial messages as well as air them, and opportunities to function similarly to a full-fledged advertising agency also exist within television stations.

Radio Stations

Radio has become particularly specialized, with stations making market-oriented decisions to go all classical or country or talk or news and weather or pop psychology or soft rock. The intent here is that by focusing on the needs of a particular market profile, the station will also be better able to attract advertisers whose products speak to that narrow market and by doing so will create a definite niche in the radio spectrum. This represents a sharp break from the past, when station programming tried to provide a little bit of everything throughout the day. Now, the trend is to provide a narrow focus and hope that it brings in a deep audience. English majors working in radio today will need to understand the particular market they are writing for so that they can communicate using language, including style, syntax, metaphors, and tone, that says to the audience, "That's talking to me!"

Specialty Advertisers

Specialty advertising is all around us. The printed yardstick from the lumberyard. The free mini-flashlight from the hardware store with the store's address and hours of operation. The credit card case imprinted with a printer's logo. Many businesses cannot afford broadcast or print media advertising, but almost every firm can afford some kind of imprinted article that reminds people who it is and where the business is located. Specialty advertising is used to complement broadcast advertising. Creative opportunities abound in this area as the specialty advertiser and the client come together to plan a promotion, event, or anniversary. Often, items, slogans, themes, and messages are expressly designed for the client. For the English major who enjoys the creative use of language, specialty advertising offers possibilities.

Outdoor Advertising Agencies

With a renewed interest in the aesthetics of public spaces, including highways, outdoor advertising has undergone some restructuring and reframing of purpose. Although restrictions proliferate, there are still ample opportunities for billboards, spectaculars, and other forms of outdoor advertising, including signs, blimps, skywriting, and tethered inflatables. Outdoor advertising specialists often work with an advertiser and its advertising agency to add outdoor ads to a complete campaign. The outdoor specialists can provide the best information on site selection, copy length, and copy/visual balance.

Magazines

Today's magazine advertising departments have assembled more information on their readership than ever before. They can tell a prospective advertiser how old their readers are, how many cars they own, how often they travel abroad, and how much money they make. The magazine uses this information to recruit the kind of advertiser its readers want to see and have need of. It will assist advertisers with designing winning appeals to the market and can advise on successful placement of the ad within the publication. Some magazine product runs allow for creative "split ads" on opposing pages or can incorporate some product samples in the assembling and stapling process.

Newspapers

Newspapers depend heavily on advertising to support the publication. Newspaper advertising departments often work very closely with clients of all sizes to assist in producing ads that are effective, often under pressures of time and space limitations. English majors interested in this particular area of employment will find their talents constantly stretched.

Public Relations Firms

Public relations organizations take on individuals, institutions (churches, corporations, not-for-profit firms, and so on), products, and even ideas and work to improve, alter, reposition, or change public opinion about them. They use every opportunity at their disposal, including the placement of news stories, photo opportunities, charity work, public appearances, and one-on-one meetings to build support for whatever position or platform they are trying to affect. Considerable written work is involved, and public relations organizations issue a steady stream of position papers, news releases, background stories, biographies, and fact sheets to support their efforts. The writing task is a demanding one, because the final product must meet severe public scrutiny.

Utilities

Another symptom of a shrinking planet and the public's interest and concern is the need for utilities to have public relations offices. Once a very quiet sector of the economy, firms that deal in oil, gasoline, natural gas, hydroelectric power, and nuclear energy are constantly being called on to explain and document their impact on the environment. In an era of rising costs that outstrip rising paychecks, there is also concern for the economic impact of ever-escalating energy costs on the individual. Public relations professionals must be excellent listeners, able to understand and empathize with others' points of view, while at the same time articulating company policy. They can play a significant role in bringing disparate viewpoints together and building bridges for cooperation. English majors looking to do PR work in the utilities need to be equally at home on the word processor and in front of the microphone. They need to be able to produce a newsletter or field angry questions from consumers. This job requires a unique blend of skilled communicator and negotiator.

Sports Organizations

Promotion of individual sports, specific sports leagues, and unique competitions are all part of the working day for public relations specialists in sports organizations. Increased attendance brings increased sponsorship and results in bigger prizes and more public attention for events. Creating excitement, raising public awareness about a sport, and attracting advertisers are all the responsibility of the sports organization public relations staff. If you have an English education and a love for sports, you may want to investigate the extensive possibilities in sports organization public relations.

Federal Government

Many job seekers would be surprised to find that the government employs public relations professionals. However, whether it's controversy surrounding federal money mismanagement, sex discrimination at a major military college, or a positive news story about military assistance during civilian disasters, the government needs qualified public relations professionals who can communicate effectively with all those interested in government activities. Because the U.S. government has numerous departments, agencies, and divisions, the entry-level public relations aspirant would do well to spend some serious investigative time on opportunities in government public relations.

State and Local Government

The same public scrutiny that necessitates federal public relations is present for state, city, and local governments to a lesser degree. Depending on the size of the locality and the issues present, the concerns may be taxes, zoning, preservation of wetlands, redistricting, highway tolls, state lotteries, and similar issues that need to be addressed in the press, on television and radio, by personal communication, and in news conferences. A high level of general information about the locality and its issues, poise under pressure, and the gift of diplomacy are all helpful attributes.

Educational Institutions

Perhaps a college campus is reacting to news reports of corporate advertising on the college's website. Or it may be a story concerning "town-gown" relations between the college and the community in which it is located. These are some of the issues a public relations staff member would be planning for and responding to in an educational institution today. Such examples are evidence of the need for the kind of skilled communications a trained professional can bring to an educational institution's relationship with the community.

Medical Institutions

Questions of medical ethics, the prolongation of life, the acceptance or denial of certain classifications of patients, the movement of patients from one facility to another, and the high-risk areas of experimental surgery and drug treatment are often the focal issues for public relations in hospital administration. Working in this field means acquiring a specialized medical vocabulary and gaining familiarity with hospital procedures because public statements must be carefully worded to avoid confusion or misstatement.

Professional Organizations

A growing number of professional associations have a critical need for a public relations practitioner. Staffs for these groups may be small and include many volunteer workers, but there is a need for skilled personnel to answer press queries and personal letters and to issue press releases on possible news stories. Some organizations find, over time, that their activities are not perceived as they desire, and they seek help to reeducate the public about their true intents and aims as an organization. Others want public support in terms of time and financial contributions and need professional help through public relations to elicit that support. Although only large, well-funded associations can maintain a professional public relations staff, this is in no way a limitation for the job seeker. Directories of associations list thousands of organizations whose size and financial structure allow them to employ PR staff.

Possible Job Titles

The two following lists are an attempt to give you some idea of possible job titles in advertising and public relations. The lists are not exhaustive. Many other titles exist that might not directly suggest an advertising or public relations function. For example, on some college campuses, there is a director of news services. A significant component of this job is public relations. Use the following lists as a rough guide, and add to them those job titles you discover through your own investigations.

Advertising
Account assistant
Account coordinator
Account director
Account or district manager
Account executive
Account specialist
Account supervisor
Account trainee
Advertising director
Art director
Assistant account executive
Assistant planner
Associate media director

Associate research director
Broadcast supervisor
Copywriter
Creative director
Executive research director
Group or regional manager
Junior account executive
Junior buyer
Management supervisor
Media buyer
Media director
Media planner
Media supervisor
Press secretary
Producer
Production assistant
Production manager
Production supervisor
Project director
Research director
Research supervisor
Researcher
Sales assistant
Sales planner
Sales representative
Traffic assistant
Traffic controller
Traffic manager

The division of these lists is somewhat arbitrary because the functions of advertising and public relations walk hand in hand most of the time. Many of these positions frequently overlap in responsibilities. Some practitioners would be hard put to tell you definitively if they are, in fact, advertising or public relations specialists because the two roles are so intertwined in some organizations. Nevertheless, the following list indicates some titles peculiar to public relations.

Public Relations
Communications specialist
Community affairs coordinator

Consumer affairs specialist
Corporate communications director
Crisis manager
Director of internal communications
Director of investor relations
Director of public affairs
Editor
Employee publications specialist
Event creation coordinator
Governmental relations staffer
Industrial public relations executive
Internal communications staffer
Investor relations officer
Media placement specialist
Media relations executive
Office of civic affairs representative
PR writer
Public affairs officer
Public information officer
Public relations assistant
Shareholder relations coordinator
Staff writer
Supervisor of educational affairs
Washington representative

Related Occupations

The fields of advertising and public relations are welcoming to the generalist such as the English major. Although the emphasis is on written and spoken communication skills, there is also a need for a high level of general information, responsiveness under pressure, the ability to present to large groups, and the ability to be endlessly responsive and creative as situations present themselves. It's difficult for an employer to know ahead of time who will be a success in this field. This brief related occupation list suggests that these skills, so valued in public relations and advertising, will be valued anywhere there is a need for someone to act as an intermediary between the organization and outside publics, formally or informally. Each of these has been selected because it draws on the same attributes to a greater or lesser degree.

Caterer
Cruise director
Development specialist
Function/special event sales manager
Fund-raiser
Interior designer
Lobbyist
Membership services director
Patient relations director
Patient relations specialist
Police officer/community relations
Promotion manager
Real estate salesperson
Religious administrator
Shopping mall manager
Spokesperson
Volunteer coordinator

Help in Locating These Employers

Advertising and public relations agencies know the value of customer awareness. As you would expect, they are masters of self-promotion. A number of
excellent websites and directories and lists are available to identify where these
employers are located, how big their staffs are, what specialties each offers,
and how much and what kind of business they do. The following list represents a beginning library of job sources for each of the possible advertising and public relations employers listed in this chapter.

- *Advertising Age* (adage.com), published by Crain Communications,
  Inc.
- *Adweek* (adweek.com), published by VNU Business Publications,
  USA, Inc., and VNU eMedia production
- *Bowker's News Media Directory: TV and Radio Directory*, published
  by R. R. Bowker
- *Careers in Advertising* by William S. Pattis, published by
  McGraw-Hill
- *Careers in Advertising and Public Relations: The WetFeet Insider
  Guide*, published by WetFeet Inc.

- *Career Opportunities in the Sports Industry* by Shelly Field, published by Checkmark Books
- *Gale Directory of Publications and Broadcast Media*, published by Thomson Gale
- *The Literary Press and Magazine Directory 2005–2006*, published by Soft Scull Press
- *O'Dwyer's Directory of Public Relations Firms* (odwyerpr.com), published by J. R. O'Dwyer Co. Inc.
- *The Public Relations Strategist*, published by the Public Relations Society of America (prsa.org)
- *Standard Directory of Advertisers 2002: Business Classifications/Index*, published by National Register Publishing
- *Standard Directory of Advertising Agencies 2003*, published by National Register Publishing
- *Vault Career Guide to Advertising* by Ira Berkowitz, published by Vault Inc.

Professional Associations for Advertising and Public Relations

The following list will begin to give you some idea of the variety and specializations of professional associations supporting the fields of advertising and public relations. As you begin your own job search, you'll find many other professional groups, some with quite specialized purposes. Their websites contain a vast amount of information. If you have additional questions, an e-mail or a telephone call to the groups often will result in them sending you materials that open up career vistas you had not imagined.

Advertising Council
261 Madison Ave.
New York, NY 10016-2303
adcouncil.org
Members/Purpose: To conduct public service advertising campaigns

Advertising Women of New York
25 West 54th St., Suite 1001
New York, NY 10036
awny.org

Members/Purpose: Professional development for women in advertising, publicity, marketing, research, or promotion
Training: Hosts annual advertising career conference
Journal/Publication: *AWNY Matters* online newsletter
Job Listings: Online job bank

American Advertising Federation
1101 Vermont Ave. NW, Suite 500
Washington, DC 20005
aaf.org
Members/Purpose: Advertisers, agencies, and media companies that comprise the nation's leading brands and corporations; promotes advertising through a nationally coordinated grassroots network of advertisers, agencies, media companies, local advertising clubs, and college chapters
Job Listings: Online job bank

American Association of Advertising Agencies
405 Lexington Ave., 18th Floor
New York, NY 10174-1801
aaaa.org
Members/Purpose: A management-oriented association that offers its members the broadest possible services, expertise, and information regarding the advertising agency business
Training: Offers Institute of Advanced Advertising Studies, variety of conferences, workshops, and programs

Association of National Advertisers
708 Third Ave.
New York, NY 10017
ana.net
Members/Purpose: National and regional advertisers
Training: Hosts conferences and regional meetings
Journal/Publication: *The Advertiser* magazine
Job Listings: Online job opportunities

Institute for Public Relations
P.O. Box 118400
2096 Weimer Hall
Gainesville, FL 32611-8400
instituteforpr.com

Members/Purpose: Includes educators/researchers, public relations
  professionals, and the corporate/institutional clients they serve; focuses
  on the science beneath the art of public relations
Training: Offers lectures and forums

**National Council for Marketing and
  Public Relations**
P.O. Box 336039
Greeley, CO 80633
ncmpr.org
Members/Purpose: Represents marketing and PR professionals at
  community, technical, and junior colleges
Training: Hosts a national conference and regional conferences
Journals/Publications: *COUNSEL* quarterly newsletter, membership
  directory, and resource guide
Job Listings: Online listing of employment opportunities

Public Relations Society of America
33 Irving Pl.
New York, NY 10003
prsa.org
Members/Purpose: Advances the standards of the public relations
  profession and provides members with professional development
  opportunities through continuing education programs, information
  exchange forums, and research projects conducted on national and local
  levels
Training: Hosts seminars and e-learning opportunities
Journals/Publications: *PRSA* e-newsletter, *The Strategist* magazine, *Tactics*
  newspaper
Job Listings: Online job center

Promotional Products Association International
3125 Skyway Circle N.
Irving, TX 75038-3526
adweb.com/adassoc33.html
Members/Purpose: Works to expand the market, establish standards,
  enhance the professionalism of the industry, and support the growth of
  member companies
Training: Hosts business academy and Webinars
Journals/Publications: *Promotional Products Business* magazine, *PPAI
  Newsletter*, *PPB Newslink* electronic newsletter

9

Path 4: Business Administration and Management

Majoring in English has been fun. Hard work, sure, but lots of fun as well: fascinating courses, interesting books, poetry, and literature to read and discuss, and the company of like-minded people who also enjoy the many forms of expression in English. You've loved all the reading and will probably spend the rest of your life as an avid reader, but how does that qualify you for a job? No one is going to pay you just to read.

Is your love of reading of any use to an employer? Absolutely! The ability to read and the enjoyment of reading are highly valued in business administration and management careers. Whether it's the mountainous volumes of memoranda, letters, magazines, or professional reading that come across a desk each day or books and articles that help one to see the big picture or learn a new management technique, all of this reading and the ability to accomplish it will come in very handy to you in management/administration. You'll be more knowledgeable, you'll have a higher level of general information, and you'll be able to refer colleagues and subordinates to information of interest to their particular concerns. Your awareness of and grasp of your reading material makes you a valuable resource, especially to others who might read less.

Writing was also very important to your degree. Short papers, long papers, documented research papers, freewriting, and journals became regular items in your bag of tricks. Unlike some students in other majors, writing became so practiced for you that these assignments were enjoyable challenges rather than onerous tasks. You became quite adept at writing under pressures of time and space limitations. You learned to condense or expand depending on what was needed or allowed. You might have even had the opportunity to contribute to a literary journal or college newspaper or help a professor with research for a scholarly article. You learned how practice and critical feedback improved your writing, and you experimented with different writing styles. You know writing is an important skill and valued by the world of work, but how exactly will you put your writing experience to work for you?

There is perhaps no single more valued gift in the world of employment than the ability to write well and easily. The amount of correspondence alone is staggering, and business writing requires an excellent vocabulary, clarity of expression, and some special stylistic techniques of directness, collaboration, and persuasion. And business writing is not lacking in opportunities for creativity, either. New business ventures, advertising proposals, international ventures, and new products all present opportunities to do something different. Not-for-profit organizations need to produce a never-ending stream of materials to help people understand and appreciate what they do and then be willing to support them. Business is constantly changing and responding to the marketplace, and business writing reflects that.

You probably found it useful in your major to know how to use word-processing software: moving texts, cutting and pasting, changing formats, and using the dictionary, thesaurus, and search-and-replace options to improve your writing presentation. Maybe you got to try your hand at some desktop publishing software as well and gained some familiarity with this popular technology. In fact, you probably saved much of your college writing output and now have a nice portfolio of work assembled and ready to print. But you don't want to be a secretary; won't your word processing and desktop publishing skills be seen as just clerical?

A quick review of available job openings for management level, college graduate positions in business administration and management, both profit and not-for-profit, display overwhelmingly the need for at least word processing competency and a variety of word processing software familiarity. Beyond this, many employers are interested in candidates having some desktop publishing skills, knowledge of graphics packages, and awareness of spreadsheet software. In the reality of the workplace, there is an overt link between the practicing business writer and communicator and the computer. Here's an excellent example of this requirement in an advertisement found on Action Without Borders (idealist.org), a specialized job posting site for the not-for-profit sector. This is the qualifications section of a want ad seeking a program assistant for a museum:

> **Requirements.** B.A., preferably in humanities. Proficiency in QuarkXPress and Adobe Photoshop, basic knowledge of HTML coding, excellent verbal and written skills, ability to work independently and to manage both short- and long-term projects, genuine interest in and some knowledge of art.

Notice the focus on the technical demands; the degree is listed first, then the technical needs that, in their specificity, overshadow the more general requirements.

Try to expand your computer skills while still in school in the areas suggested and, if you have graduated, see about some continuing education courses in desktop publishing or spreadsheet analysis software. Don't let this kind of easily acquired technological skill come between you and a job that lets you use many of your English major skills.

Here's another advertisement, for a project analyst for a financial services company:

> **Project Analyst.** Responsibilities: data management, event budgets, cost analysis, RFP (request for proposal) development, reporting, and maintaining program calendars. Skills: very good computer skills, including Microsoft Outlook, Word, Excel and PowerPoint; great organizational skills; keen attention to detail and follow-up; self-motivated; and possess strong communication and writing skills. Bachelor's degree required.

Certainly a B.A. in English would be acceptable, but that is hardly enough to be competitive. Familiarity with budgeting, organizing data, and report writing is also required. This is an excellent example of the kinds of demands an employer believes it can make on a college graduate today. The degree by itself is simply not enough for this organization.

Maybe your interest is in business, not in teaching, but you had some great teachers who taught you to listen, to express yourself in a complete and reasoned way, and to understand that being critical is not being negative, but rather evaluative. This evaluative skill will be particularly useful in business, where much work is done in groups and individuals come to the table with differing perspectives. There may be someone who will look at a proposal from a quantitative perspective. Another may bring the history of the organization to bear on a situation. Yet another may have a public relations or marketing approach. You may look at the logic, the tone, and the bigger picture of the concept and bring a valuable and completely different perspective to the situation.

Your teachers taught you about styles, periods, and the nuances of particular writers. You learned from them the value and power of specific choices in vocabulary. From hour upon hour in the classroom you came to appreciate the well-developed lecture or thoughtful presentation and understand the mechanics of public presentation skills. You will frequently find yourself called upon in meetings, both with and without advance notice, to speak on certain subjects, sometimes at length. The modeling you received from your classroom presentations is sure to influence your own presentation style. You'll understand how to speak to the audience and what audience members are interested in hearing. You will have learned to modulate your voice and include everyone with eye contact. You'll have a sense of when visual aids would be a compelling addition to a presentation.

Do writing and reading and word processing skills open any doors for you? Absolutely! If there is one constant refrain from the world of organized business, large and small, it is "We need people who can think and speak and write—we'll teach them everything else they need." English majors, take a look at administration and management careers.

Definition of the Career Path

Because an English degree program focuses on educating the student about the traditions of the English language and its contemporary reflection in modern literature, poetry, theater, video, art, and film, it's common for an English major to have an immensely successful college career, graduate with honors, and yet feel ill-equipped to find a good job. We've indicated that although some wonderful skills and training have been received, it's necessary for the job seeker to learn to extract those skills from the context of an education in English and transform them in a way an employer will find attractive.

This means taking a skill out of the academic context, for example, writing research papers on topics in English literature. For the business employer who isn't in need of English-literature research writing, that particular skill may be difficult to fully appreciate. Some employers would do the necessary generalization and understand its value, but it's more effective and certain if you do it. So instead of indicating on your résumé that you know how to write and research papers on subjects in English literature, you might better indicate that you are comfortable with research methods and resources. You can assemble pertinent data on a subject using a variety of reference materials and transform that data into a piece of valuable information. Now, the employer thinks, "Yes, that is something I can use." It's easy to do!

The best way to begin to understand how valuable your English degree might be to the world of administration and management is to review some current job postings. Look at Internet job listings and Sunday papers with want ads. It doesn't matter if they are out of date; you're reviewing them to learn how employers request people with your kind of talent. These job postings will educate you in a couple of different ways. What phrases do they use, and what kinds of skills do they expect? Where do your talents match up with what's requested, and where do you fall short? Some will directly ask for English skills; others will speak of writing and verbal presentation ability. As you read the job descriptions, you will begin to become familiar with menus of duties and responsibilities you might be performing. Another bonus of this exercise is that you will discover job titles. Even when we have a good idea about what we want to do with our lives and the employment environment we want to find ourselves in, we often don't know what they call what we want to do. This exercise helps you to learn about and build your own personal library of job titles to explore. And if you need further information on any particular job, you can research it in the *O*NET Dictionary of Occupational Titles* (http://online.onetcenter.org).

Your college career office or library may have some additional job posting newsletters with listings of entry-level jobs for liberal arts graduates in a number of fields directly and indirectly related to English. Check those out as well.

Following is an excellent example of a position for which English majors would be well qualified but that they might not be aware of or might not expect to refer to skills they possess.

Program Manager. Plans and administers work on large projects having a significant business or global impact on the organization. Develops detailed project plans and analyses, researches and identifies key barriers/problems, monitors and tracks progress. Entry-level professional contributor, requires B.A./B.S. and zero to two years of experience, excellent communication skills, familiarity with databases and GIS.

This kind of job could exist in both the commercial and not-for-profit sectors and within each of them in numerous kinds of organizations: medical, sales, agriculture, or banking, just to name a few.

We've established that the English major is well-grounded in analytical skills and should have solid writing and communication skills. So you fit the bill for the example position on that score. Your research experience would have allowed you training in the kind of tracking and reporting of data that is being requested in this advertisement. The subject matter may be different, but the procedures and evaluative process are identical. It's just a new vocabulary.

Certainly the advertisement is not requesting anything outside the range of the average English major, except perhaps some software familiarity. As we have mentioned, computer skills have been stressed throughout all the English-major career paths cited, so if time remains in your degree, use that time to acquire as many computer skills as you can in desktop publishing, spreadsheet programs, word processing, and databases. It will stand you in good stead in the employment market.

Here's another example, again with some computer skills required and a specific interest in publishing.

Communications Project Manager. Large corporation with multiple internal communications departments and a wide variety of projects. Something new every day: event planning, strategizing with internal clients, executing communications projects, some writing. Must be a born multitasker with a lot of patience and confidence for dealing with all corporate levels and personalities. Bachelor's degree and strong writing abilities, knowledge of Word and Excel, experience with project management software a plus.

This ad may seem typical of what you would expect for an English major seeking entry-level employment. It focuses on communications (even in the job title), and it involves writing. But publishing is not the only place for such a communications project management job. The clone of the job could exist in the sciences, medical, financial, or management research fields and in U.S. government positions as well. The material you would be working with would be different in each area, but the tasks and processes would be similar.

Management trainee ads for any number of employers often simply ask for a four-year graduate because they are looking for a broad range of skills and will do most of the specialized training in company and product awareness on the job. They prefer college graduates for their education, intelligence, and exposure to a broad range of subject fields. They especially appreciate English majors for their emphasis on communication skills. Jobs as diverse as production assistant for a TV station, sales account manager in industry, research associate, political campaign manager, assistant director for personnel services, and a host of equally interesting and varied positions seek an English or other appropriate four-year degree. Each requires good written and verbal communication skills, analytical ability, perhaps some research experience, and almost always computer literacy and often familiarity with particular software.

So you will certainly be using the skills you practiced in acquiring your degree and some new ones besides. The context won't be literature, but it almost certainly will be prose, and you will play a major role in ensuring that writing is clear, direct, correct, and has some style as well. Letters, memoranda, policies, procedures, and short and long business reports are the currency of the workplace. The quality of this writing is a direct reflection on the organization sponsoring it. Consequently, individuals who can write, edit, and present these materials are valued for those skills.

Here's a fund-raising position with an emphasis on issues and skills and not on the particular degree:

Development Officer. Assist development director by drafting fund raising appeals and brochures, researching prospective donors, and visiting donors. Must be respectful of confidential conversations. Possess excellent communications skills and computer skills including word processing/spreadsheet. Requires B.A./B.S, fund-raising experience helpful.

Think about the different talents you are developing in your English major and try to picture yourself using them in some employment context. Which do you enjoy the most and which the least? Which must be part of a job and which will you not miss? The study of English as a major is comprehensive enough to ready you for a variety of worthwhile occupations in which you can justifiably say you are using your degree to the fullest.

In your job as a manager or administrator, you'll eventually begin to have people under your leadership, and you will be involved in staff supervision, perhaps some budgetary control, and evaluation of your staff. From time to time there'll be hiring decisions as well. These are all important skills in any job, and all require leaving a "paper trail": a formal letter offering someone a position, a sick leave or vacation time policy, a proposal for reorganizing a department or division, or introducing a new product to an existing product line.

Even if you feel assured from reading this book that an employer needs your skills, you might recognize that your education in English seldom focused on the world of employment. You had opportunities to listen to poets and novelists read their work. You might have had a journalist visit your class. But did you ever have a visit from a manager/administrator who wanted to share with you how he or she uses his or her degree in English? Probably not. You legitimately feel somewhat ill-informed about the world of business. What do various organizations do? What are the functions of different departments and the roles of the people who staff those departments? As you go about your job search, you'll want to fill in the gaps in your knowledge about business by doing some basic research about organizations and specific firms. With your educational background, this will not be a problem for you!

Company literature can be a goldmine of information about organizational structure. Internet sites, brochures, and pamphlets describe departments, show organizational charts, and may contain photographs of individuals at work. Some organizations break down along functional lines: accounting, personnel, finance, and marketing. Others use their products as the division: boilers, generators, transformers, or cables.

If, for example, you are looking at a management trainee position for a fruit juice manufacturer, you could check out the food processing industry on the Internet or at your library or college career center. Learn about the basic operation of the industry, possible departments, staffing, and raw materials sourcing. Next seek out information about the particular company that you are applying to.

Organizations such as Veryfine, Snapple, or Ocean Spray describe their products and their manufacturing process. Some firms publish human resources brochures that profile selected workers and their jobs. These descriptions can give you an even better sense of what this organization does and who works there.

As you begin to realize how widely attractive the English major is to many kinds of employers, you'll soon build up quite a knowledge base about certain fields. You can then focus your research more on specific organizations and less on the sector they are part of. Becoming so aware of the world of employment is part of any job search, but for the English major, there are many more doors available to open and, consequently, more to learn.

Perhaps you chose English as a degree simply because you love to read and think. These corporate jobs sound interesting to you, and it may be comforting to realize that so much of American business would value your skills. But some of these jobs may sound more active, more extroverted than fits your personality. They suggest lots of interpersonal communication, high degrees of interaction, and potentially some conflict or dissonance. You worry that perhaps, although you have the skills, the environment will be wrong. Are there corporate jobs for people who like to just read and think?

The answer to this reasonable question is a complicated one. First, there are jobs in business, industry, and nonprofits that involve significant amounts of reading and thinking. That work may be solitary and introverted as the reader wrestles with concepts or ideas. Ultimately, however, the results of such work must be presented publicly, either to a supervisor, a committee, or a team. That presentation may be verbal, written, or a combination of techniques.

The kinds of jobs that are this autonomous and self-directed are almost always fairly senior positions in terms of rank and salary. It would be unusual in an entry-level position to just send the new employee off to read or think with no understanding of the organization and its mission, goals, or history.

With such senior responsibility (and commensurate salary) come additional duties beyond one's primary task of reading and thinking. The organization has the right to use the skills of this thinker/reader for the general good. It would demand that this good thinking be brought to bear on decision making and goal setting. So while such positions do exist, they exist at senior levels for experienced staff who often have other equally important ancillary duties that put them on the line again and again.

Working Conditions

Corporate working conditions and norms of behavior may also inspire some hesitation. You may sense that business and industry and even some larger, more organized not-for-profit organizations have more rules about conduct, appearance, manners, and hierarchy than you have been used to or would enjoy. After all, part of your decision to major in English might have been a rejection of some of the same work orientation or profit motive that led some of your peers to major in business or computer science. Now you're also considering the world of commerce and justifiably wondering, will I fit in?

Rest assured that the world of work is as diverse as the population in general. It is filled with people of differing interests, political persuasions, lifestyles, values, and talents. There is certainly room for you. Your skills are valued and needed, and most organizations realize that along with your talent and education comes a particular philosophy and lifestyle.

But that is not to suggest that some changes will not have to be made. After all, a corporation is a public entity represented by its employees. How they look, act, and communicate affects the business and, ultimately, their livelihood. Publicly traded companies with shareholders may feel this responsibility to a greater degree than does a private company or family-held business. Nevertheless, a business's success rises and falls on its ability to maintain good relations with its publics.

Businesses today have become much more sophisticated about their staff and their needs. Some offer flexible time scheduling with varying arrival and departure times for different workers. Some will allow two people to share a job, each person taking on a specific set of duties. This kind of benefit has been helpful for parents who are interested in staying home more with young children. Some larger organizations offer on-site child-care or elder-care—a real recognition of home and scheduling problems. An increasing number of firms are offering benefits to gay couples and recognizing same-sex couples in invitations to social functions. Firms often offer counseling and referral services for a variety of problems and do so discreetly and without the stigma these problems earned employees in corporations of the past.

Many firms now offer memberships in health or fitness clubs or have those kinds of facilities on-site as part of their benefits program. Of course, this emphasis on exercise and diet has beneficial effects on productivity and reduced absenteeism. Even more than that, it builds self-esteem; people become prouder of how they look and feel and return that pride in their work. It increases camaraderie and cuts across all hierarchical lines as different kinds of workers meet in the gym and weight room.

Many organizations offer trips to the ballet, theater, sports events, and museum openings for employees and their families at greatly reduced prices. You are sure to find many like-minded individuals at work and have many opportunities to share your enthusiasms and interests in work-sponsored activities.

It might be easy to believe that because a nonprofit organization is involved in doing good in the world, many of the conditions so entrenched in a corporation would not exist in the not-for-profit. Although some nonprofit organizations do have relaxed norms, a great many others know that to gain the private and public dollars needed to run these organizations and inspire public trust, they need to present in every way the same picture of organization, sophistication, and determination as a corporation.

Another reasonable concern is the issue of competitiveness. Are corporate climates as competitive as they are portrayed to be? Certainly as an English major you competed for grades and to better your own past performance, but you were also in a sense competing with a class standard set by all members. Business is no different. While most competitive initiative is outwardly directed toward other firms, there are certainly performance norms established over time by the general level of expertise in the firm. Because you are hired in large part with these norms in mind, and your résumé and experience were evaluated on criteria already established for success in the organization, you will probably do fine. What is important is that you stay "tuned in" as an employee to performance standards and do your best to maintain your contributions.

You will participate in periodic evaluations with your direct supervisor to review your accomplishments and set appropriate goals for yourself for the next evaluation period. These evaluations will be the proper setting to discuss your understanding and appreciation of your job, your desire for additional training, or your ideas for job modification.

Training and Qualifications

Our review of some sample advertisements has made it clear that along with your fine English education, some computer familiarity would be well advised. It is impossible to anticipate all the potential demands of the marketplace, but certainly word processing, some spreadsheet software, some personal computer hardware familiarity, and desktop publishing techniques would be attractive additions to your résumé. If you have some of the skills on this list, you would at least be able to negotiate to learn the rest on the job. Without any of these skills, an employer has no way of judging whether you are computer literate or whether you will turn out to be difficult to train. If you have at least some computer experience, there is less risk in spending training dollars on your computer education as an employee.

If your curriculum allows, a general introduction to business course would also be helpful, especially if it touches on accounting principles, management, and operations. This information would help you to understand your employer's situation, improve your communication at interviews, and speed up your research activities when investigating certain industries or specific companies. Some schools offer an introduction to not-for-profit organizations, which would be of help to anyone interested in that employment sector.

Any kind of business internship would also assure an employer of your interest in applying your English skills in the public arena. You might look at internships in communications, research, office administration, development, membership services, event coordination, program planning, or in rotating assignments where you have the opportunity to spend some time in all the departments of an organization. You'll come away from such an experience with a strong sense of what you could do for a firm and how an organization functions.

Earnings

This is a broad employment category, and starting salaries are a function of both the general salaries in the industry you are looking at (salaries in industry will be higher than in service firms) and your particular set of skills. The more specific skills (computer, math, research, and others) you bring in addition to your degree, the higher your initial salary range. According to the National Association of Colleges and Employers (jobweb.com), entry-level salaries range from $31,200 to $36,491.

Career Outlook

The kinds of positions we have been discussing are sometimes referred to as *generalist* positions. They are not technical jobs, and the educational background required is rather broad. Additionally, with these generalist positions there are no firmly established criteria for entry-level positions. Much depends on the employer being approached and the particular combination of skills, talent, and personality of the applicant and how that combination fits. The hiring outlook has much to do with the general trend of the economy and the size and location of the hiring organization, as well. These types of positions often follow trends. If, for example, an industry and the employers within that sector are not doing well, the funds employers have to spend on hiring new employees will probably first go toward technical expertise to improve efficiency and product quality and then to financial management staff to ensure fiscal control and solvency. The newly degreed general administrator with "soft" or untried skills is not an attractive commodity at such times.

When personnel staffing funds are more freely available, it is easier to find and win these positions. A corollary of this is that these positions are also more likely to be early casualties during a downturn in the economy through layoffs, reductions in force, enforced leaves of absence, or outright dismissals. To prevent this situation, you are encouraged to use your employed time to acquire more specific skills that would significantly alter your résumé.

A good example of this would be how you self-manage for growth in an entry-level position as a human resources associate for a large company. Perhaps you have been hired as an assistant benefits administrator, briefing new employees on benefit program choices and assisting in managing the smooth flow of paperwork and forms surrounding the filing and paying of claims. You could do this job in an exemplary manner for three years and yet still only be qualified for an identical job somewhere else.

Or you could request cross-training in OSHA (Occupational Safety and Health Administration) guidelines for workers, participate in professional development programs to learn more about pay classification guidelines, volunteer to work on the team producing a new benefits brochure and pick up copywriting and graphics experience, and participate in every training opportunity provided. Ask your boss if you can sit in on contract negotiations when benefits packages are up for renewal. Soon you will discover you have built a substantial body of expertise in your field. No longer are you a generalist with only your degree to recommend you; now you are qualified as a payroll specialist, benefits officer, employee trainer, or even director of personnel for a smaller organization.

Strategy for Finding the Jobs

As an English major seeking employment in the areas of business administration and management, you need to do three things to be successful. First, you need to become skillful at transforming descriptions of your academic skills and successes into skills and attributes that the workplace will find valuable. Second, you must know who the employers are. Third, you must reflect what you have learned on your résumé, in your cover letter, and in your interview comments.

Help Businesses Appreciate Your Skills

Candidates need to be able to document each of their strengths with anecdotes and examples that will have meaning to an employer who is far removed from the world of college academics. So if one of your particularly strong skills is project planning, you will want to express that to the employer as a usable skill. Perhaps you acquired project planning skills in terms of research paper writing or end-of-semester presentations. This won't make much of an impact on an employer. But if you suggest to the employer that you have project planning skills that can help in opening new branches or making client presentations or preparing for a sales conference, that will have more impact. You can then talk about attention to detail, assembling all relevant materials, coordinating with involved staff, and producing the necessary ancillary materials. You have taken your skills out of one context and placed them in another.

Know Something About the Organizations You Are Contacting

The second ingredient for success follows naturally from the first. To convincingly express the importance of your skills to a business employer, you will need to know something about the organization's product, personnel, and operations. It has always been a watchword of the job search process to know something about the employer you are contacting for work. This is especially important for the generalist coming from an English major to work in business or administration. It's up to you, not the employer, to express where in the organization you can be most effective and what kinds of contributions you can make. You cannot do that effectively without understanding your potential employer's operation.

Obtain company literature from the firm's home page or from your college career office. In addition to annual reports, you'll find product line information, human resources literature, and statements of philosophy of business and mission. Look at more general sources, including current periodicals, to gain a sense of current strengths and challenges to the industry. As an English major, you know the value of specialized vocabularies from reading Shakespeare or Dickens. Entering the world of business and administration requires the same kind of diligent application to feel at home.

Reflect Newfound Knowledge on Your Résumé, Cover Letter, and in Interviews

It is especially important for the English major's résumé to say to a business audience, "I'm trained to contribute to your organization." You can do this in the way you describe your objective and history. Use the tips we've described here to set yourself apart from other liberal arts students who haven't figured out that their résumé should focus on their audience rather than on themselves. Your cover letter needs to confirm your understanding of the business world, and you must be ready to discuss the relevance of your degree and experience during the job interview.

Possible Employers

It is no exaggeration to say that the accomplished English graduate holds a degree that is an accepted passport across the borders of every industry. Employers know and value the educational background of an individual who has studied English in college. Moreover, they appreciate the contribution that such an individual can make to their organization.

Let's take the world of work and divide it up into some general categories. We'll profile each of these sectors for you and provide both general and specific resources to help you explore on your own. You'll be looking for employers that are doing things you're interested in and who hire people in the job title categories you've identified.

Not-for-Profit Organizations
All too often, the words *employment, job,* and *career* fail to call up images that include the large and diversified group of employers in the not-for-profit sector. Many of these simply cannot afford to spend for advertising what their counterparts do in the for-profit zone. Often, because these organizations benefit by and are supported by targeted markets, such advertising would not be a wise expenditure. Nevertheless, it would behoove the job seeker to investigate this rich and varied group of employers.

Not-for-profit employers can be segmented into the following broad categories:

- Arts, culture, and humanities
- Education
- Environment
- Animal related
- Health care
- Mental health and crisis intervention
- Voluntary health associations and medical disciplines
- Medical research
- Crime and legal related
- Employment

- Food, agriculture, and nutrition
- Housing and shelter
- Public safety, disaster preparedness, and relief
- Recreation and sports
- Youth development
- Human services
- International, foreign affairs, and national security
- Civil rights, social action, and advocacy
- Community improvement and capacity building
- Philanthropy, voluntarism, and grant making
- Science and technology
- Social science
- Public and societal benefit
- Religion related
- Mutual and membership benefit

An incredible range of concerns have precipitated the formation of innumerable not-for-profit organizations. Just a few of these issues are animal rights, government funding for the arts, child advocacy, consumer advocacy, education, energy use and the environment, government oversight, homelessness, hunger, legal aid, influence of the media, peace and disarmament, people with disabilities, social action, social work, sustainable agriculture, and women's issues.

Where You Might Fit In. A common characteristic of small not-for-profit organizations is that one employee may wear many hats. This means that when an organization hires a worker for one job, it seeks someone who can fill other roles as well. So an administrator may be called on at various times to serve as a trainer or an editor or a telemarketer. The English major is versatile, and not-for-profit employers will find that especially attractive.

For the English major or graduate seeking employment, these nonprofit organizations offer as many opportunities as the commercial sector. Not-for-profits have a similar organizational structure, including positions relating to the following administrative functions: human resources, office management, field staff direction, accounting, public relations, government relations, legislative relations, marketing, membership services, management information systems, development, outreach, and volunteer management.

Help in Locating These Employers. A personnel professional in the not-for-profit sector recommends that job seekers investigate policy changes, grant-making trends, and local initiatives to stand the best chance of finding job openings. One place to begin is at jobsatnonprofits.com. The company that sponsors the site is a well-known software and services supplier to nonprofits. Another good site is published by the *Chronicle of Philanthropy* and is called PhilanthropyCareers (http://philanthropy.com/jobs). Both sites allow you to search by location, keyword, and job title.

Some other organizations that can provide information include the Foundation Center (http://fdncenter.org), National Training and Information Center (ntic-us.org), Environmental Support Center (envsc.org), and Society for Nonprofit Organizations (snpo.org).

Institutions of Higher Education

Institutions of higher education can be reasonably included in any not-for-profit listing, but they deserve their own category for several reasons. First, they encompass a vast range of employment levels from gardeners to professors. Second, they value skill and care in written and spoken English because it is a reflection of the institution. And finally, they are often both institutions of learning and complete communities that produce an enormous range of activities, programs, and literature, providing unusual scope in terms of job titles and activities.

Where You Might Fit In. Junior and community colleges, vocational/technical colleges, and four-year colleges and universities are all institutions of higher education, and they offer many entry level jobs that require at least a bachelor's degree. These jobs are found in the student services, development, and business units of schools. Consider this range of departments: admissions and records, career planning and placement, commuter student programs, counseling, financial aid, international student programs, judicial programs, minority student services, orientation programs, residential life programs, student activities and organizations, student union, business, development, and alumni relations.

The size of the institution will affect the number of positions available in these units; you can expect that larger colleges and universities will hire many staff members to meet the needs of their students, faculty, and staff.

Help in Locating These Employers. Each of these categories of academic institution is easily located, and a number of resources provide classifications by school size, type, academic majors offered, size of student population, and geographic locale. As a result, they are relatively easy to identify for your job search. Some of the standard reference sources through which you may locate academic employers include job listings in the *Chronicle of Higher Education* (chronicle.com), *Peterson's Undergraduate Guide: Four Year Colleges 2006* and *Peterson's Graduate Guide Set 2005* (petersons.com), which lists schools offering graduate programs.

Professional Organizations

As you may have noticed in reading this book, there is an association or professional organization to support every possible human endeavor. Reading through a directory of associations can be fascinating, educational, alarming, and amusing as you encounter groups of people organized around other people (James Dean Memory Club), products (North Atlantic Seafood Association), activities (Foreign Car Haters Club of America), political persuasions (Monarchist Alliance), and job categories (Academy of Dispensing Audiologists) that meet the needs and interests of nearly any type of worker. There are more than thirty-five thousand professional associations and societies. Nearly every association of this type has a not-for-profit structure, but because there are so many professional associations, they deserve separate attention.

Where You Might Fit In. The activities of most of these organizations revolve around year-round direct mail correspondence with their members punctuated by regularly scheduled conferences or annual meetings. Many organizations also publish directories, journals, and newsletters. Consequently, there are significant employment opportunities in preparing written materials: regularly scheduled letters and mailings to members, newsletters and newspapers, informational packets and membership services brochures to potential members, meeting packets, and educational materials.

Additionally, these organizations hear from nonmembers seeking information and answers to questions about the organization, its members, and its aims. Home pages, pamphlets, and brochures are often made available to answer these questions. Some even have targeted career information available for their industry.

In reading through the entries shown for each organization in a reference such as the *Directory of Associations, National Organizations of the U.S.*, or *Regional, State, and Local Organizations*, look for the number of staff members employed there. Entries will indicate publications and services as well. Also be sure to read about the purpose of the group to see whether it is something you are interested in. Many people who work for professional organizations are expected to feel strongly about what the organization is trying to accomplish.

Help in Locating These Employers. If you haven't visited a career library or the career section of a public library, be sure to do so, and look for the titles listed previously or *National Trade and Professional Associations of the United States.* All of these resources list organizations that need workers with the skills you have to offer. They have a geographic index to allow you to locate potential employers in any state you are hoping to live in.

Federal Government

The federal government, even with budget cutbacks, is still the largest employer in the country, hiring about 2 percent of the nation's civilian work force. Federal government jobs can be found in every state and in large metropolitan areas. Future budget cutbacks will affect the number of entry-level government positions available, and competition for those jobs will be keen, but there continues to be a need for federal employees.

Most federal government agencies hire graduates who are considered generalists. Some of the agencies include the Air Force; U.S. Army Information Systems Engineering Command; U.S. Army Training and Doctrine Command; Bureau of Alcohol, Tobacco, and Firearms; Bureau of Labor Statistics; Employment and Training Administration; Employment Standards Administration; Equal Employment Opportunity Commission; Federal Aviation Administration; Federal Deposit Insurance Corporation; Federal Highway Administration; General Services Administration; U.S. Citizenship and Immigration Services; Department of Labor; Library of Congress; Maritime Administration; Surface Deployment and Distribution Command; Mine Safety and Health Administration; National Science Foundation; Occupational Safety and Health Administration; Office of Inspector General; Office of Personnel Management; Health and Human Services; Railroad Retirement Board; Department of State; U.S. Marshals Service; U.S. Postal Service; and Department of Veterans Affairs.

Where You Might Fit In. Each of these government units has an organizational structure that provides job opportunities ranging from generalist to specialist. The Library of Congress, for example, hires people with Ph.D.s in biology for biological science analyst positions and people with B.A.s in the liberal arts as research assistants; the General Services Administration looks for English majors to work as contract specialists and seeks law-degree holders to work as attorneys.

Many of these federal government agencies have their own administrative staff responsible for various functions including personnel, procurement, and reporting. Some resources to help familiarize you with the operations of these various units include *A Guide to America's Federal Jobs: A Complete Directory of U.S. Government Career Opportunities, Federal Jobs: The Ultimate Guide,* and *Government Job Finder: Where the Jobs Are in Local, State, and Federal Government.*

Help in Locating These Employers. A good place to start looking for actual job listings is on the U.S. government's website, usajobs.opm.gov. This site explains the federal employment process and lets you look at current job openings, get general information on federal agencies, and submit an online application.

If you select the option "Search Jobs" and then enter the keywords "entry-level professional," you can begin exploring the possibilities. Or select options relating to job type, geographic area, and date of job listing. Submit your search criteria, then select any of the entries and a detailed job description will be provided, including information on whom to contact for more information and how to apply for the specific position.

State and Local Government
State and local governments offer a variety of administrative positions in departments that include corrections, court systems, education, fire protection, health, highway and street construction, housing and community development, hospitals, libraries, natural resources, parks and recreation, police, sanitation, transportation, utilities, and welfare and human services.

Where You Might Fit In. As with the federal government, there is a range of agencies and job titles that you should consider. Many specialists are hired, but generalists such as the English major will fit in comfortably in many places. The book *Government Job Finder: Where the Jobs Are in Local, State, and Federal Government* details the many possibilities.

Help in Locating These Employers. Use your favorite search engine and enter "State of (put state name here)." You will find references to state departments; look for Employment, Personnel, or Human Resources, then look for job listings, opportunities, and so on. You will also find application procedures and contact names, and some sites will allow you to apply online.

For-Profit Businesses
If you have or are getting a degree in English and you are thinking about working in a for-profit setting, the possibilities for employment occur in every area of human endeavor. You may not have considered some of these indus-

tries: agriculture, forestry, fishing, mining, construction, manufacturing, transportation, public utilities, wholesale trade, retail trade, finance, insurance, real estate, and business and personal services.

You may find it difficult to imagine all the possible categories of employment available to you, so here's an easy exercise. Pick up your local yellow pages telephone directory. Advertisers are listed under general headings: contractors, desktop publishing services, hospitals, mortgage services, paper manufacturers, resorts, transportation, and video production services. A walk through the phone book is a reminder of all the employment possibilities around us that are duplicated in nearly every locality.

Where You Might Fit In. For-profit employers spend most of their energy in connecting their product or service with a potential market. The essence of that connection is communication. Of course, this may involve written and verbal communication as well as the media. But even more than public communications, there is a demand for individual talent to focus and define an organization's mission, to clarify goals, to set agendas, and to enunciate strategies to reach those goals.

A never-ending stream of both public external and private internal communications is the hallmark of the for-profit employer. The employer has a message, a product, or a service that must be communicated clearly to an audience if the business is to survive. The business has the opportunity to improve the quality and delivery of that product, whatever it may be. The English major who can write and speak clearly, who can analyze and solve problems, who can do research and transform data into meaningful information, and who can persuade people to take action is vitally important to organizations in this sector of the economy.

Because these organizations must continually respond to the marketplace, the English major can expect to be stretched, to grow, to be challenged, and to play a major role in the ever-changing definition of the competitive organization.

Help in Locating These Employers. If you're looking locally or regionally and are including small and midsize organizations in your search, begin with your paper telephone book or an online telephone directory. Search the Web for a local chamber of commerce—most sites include member directories, the state Department of Business and Industry, and the regional Small Business Administration.

For more comprehensive searches and to include major employers, you'll want to consult some of the larger directories published for just such a purpose. These include *Ward's Business Directory of U.S. Private and Public Companies, Lexis Nexis Corporate Affiliations* (your library may have an electronic version of this), *Business Rankings Annual,* and *Hoover's Handbook of American Business.*

Possible Job Titles

Whether an organization is a for-profit or a not-for-profit entity, you will see similar job titles, because there are basic functions necessary to run both types of organizations. Watch for advertisements for jobs such as:

Account representative
Communications assistant
Field staff director
Marketing manager
Office manager
Personnel officer
Production assistant
Program manager
Project director
Public relations assistant
Research assistant

Some job titles that may be seen more frequently in the nonprofit sector include:

Counselor
Director of volunteers
Event manager
Membership coordinator
Outreach worker

Don't be frightened off by the title of counselor. Many nonprofit organizations are seeking people with a willingness to learn these skills in addition to people who may already possess them. Sometimes, however, a counseling job really doesn't involve counseling in the strict sense of the word.

There are some jobs, like office manager or administrative assistant, that many people associate with secretarial work. In fact, there are many highly paid people in these types of jobs who do very little secretarial work, for example, managers of large medical facilities or law firms. You may want to look more closely at the job descriptions for this type of work the next time you review job postings.

In higher education, often-seen job titles unique to the functions of a college or university that are associated with student affairs divisions include:

Admissions representative
Career adviser
Program coordinator
Administrative aide
Financial aid representative
International student coordinator
Minority student programmer
Orientation coordinator
Residential life adviser
Student activities coordinator
Student union administrator
Special programs coordinator

The business division of a college or university would include job titles such as:

Development associate
Financial aid officer
Grants administrator
Technical assistant
Trainer

Any government unit, whether at the federal, state, city, or local level, is involved in such a wide range of activities that it would be difficult to enumerate all of the possible job titles. The following list is provided as a teaser:

Outdoor recreation planner
Public-health program specialist
Technical writer
Appraiser
Communications specialist
Financial examiner
Industrial specialist
Traffic manager

Computer specialist
Personnel manager
Contract representative
Import specialist
Archivist
Geographer
Social scientist
Park ranger

If you would like to gain a deeper understanding of the range of possible job titles, start by reviewing the *Occupational Outlook Quarterly*. Use the industry index in the *O*NET Dictionary of Occupational Titles* to expand your list of interesting job titles in the various industries. Before long, you'll have a much deeper understanding of the range of possible job titles that you are interested in and qualified to apply for.

Professional Associations for Business and Administration

A variety of associations are listed here. We have tried to include at least one for each of the types of employers described.

Alliance for Nonprofit Management
1899 L Street NW, 6th Floor
Washington, DC 20036
allianceonline.org
Members/Purpose: Devoted to improving the management and governance
    capacity of nonprofits—to assist nonprofits in fulfilling their mission
Journals/Publications: *Pulse!* bimonthly e-mail newsletter, *Enhance*
    newsletter
Job Listings: Online career bank

American Federation of State, County, and
    Municipal Employees
1625 L St. NW
Washington, DC 20036
afscme.org
Members/Purpose: AFL-CIO public service employees union

Journals/Publications: *AFSCME Leader*, public newsletter, women's newsletter
Job Listings: Employment opportunities listed online

National Association of Government Employees
159 Burgin Pkwy.
Quincy, MA 02169
nage.org
Members/Purpose: National union of civilian federal government employees with locals and members in military agencies, the Internal Revenue Service, Postal Service, Veterans Administration, General Services Administration, Federal Aviation Administration, and other federal agencies, as well as state and local agencies

National Business Association
5151 Beltline Rd., Suite 1150
Dallas, TX 75254
nationalbusiness.org
Members/Purpose: Assists the self-employed and small business community in achieving their professional goals
Training: Sponsors seminars
Journal/Publication: *Biz Corner* weekly e-newsletter

Society for Non-Profit Organizations
5820 Canton Center Rd., Suite 165
Canton, MI 48187
snpo.org
Members/Purpose: Executive directors, staff, board members, volunteers, and other professionals who serve nonprofit organizations; promotes excellence in leadership, management, and governance practices
Training: Sponsors seminars and workshops on nonprofit management and leadership; offers online Learning Institute
Journal/Publication: *Nonprofit World* magazine
Job Listings: Links to online job listings

U.S. Chamber of Commerce
1615 H St. NW
Washington, DC 20062-2000
uschamber.com

Members/Purpose: Businesses of all sizes and sectors—from large Fortune 500 companies to home-based, one-person operations; advances human progress through an economic, political, and social system based on individual freedom, incentive, initiative, opportunity, and responsibility
Training: Offers wide variety of educational and networking programs
Journals/Publications: *USChamber.com* monthly publication, weekly e-newsletter
Job Listings: Online search of job postings

Path 5:
Technical Writing

We live in an increasingly technological age. Technology changes the speed at which we communicate, the devices we use to communicate, and even the language we employ to express ourselves. Cell phones, pagers, answering machines, fax machines, word processors, videophones, and portable computers have all dramatically altered the movement of words, ideas, and images. Not only is there more information to deal with each day, but we may also need help both to acquire the information we need and to interpret the information we have.

Most of us see only the commercial and consumer-oriented products of this technological revolution. But there is an industrial revolution of even greater magnitude going on as well: one state is exploring the use of "smart" levees wired with control systems of electronic sensors. They sound alarms if a weakening levee threatens to breach, giving crews time to make emergency repairs; firms providing the latest in biometric security, using systems that can identify an individual's face, hand, or fingerprint, are enjoying a boom amid an increase in forgery and cybercrime. Systems like these need to be managed just as any human workforce does.

In addition to our own active participation in this revolution, we rely on words, both written and spoken, to explain the world to us. But what happens when the world becomes so complicated that words aren't sufficient to help us understand or the words themselves are almost like a foreign language?

We need a new kind of interpreter, someone who can take the complex and make it digestible for those of us without a technical background. We need an intermediary between this increasingly technocratic world and our own lives. But we also need people who can communicate in these new technical languages, people who write, speak, and communicate with each other in dialects of their own devising to continue producing the products, services, and enhancements of life that come with technology. These are technical writers.

Definition of the Career Path

The term *technical writing* is subject to various interpretations. Anyone close to the field will have his or her own favorite definition of the job and its duties. Two interpretations seem to be among the most prevalent. One states that technical writers are responsible for taking material that is difficult for the layperson to understand and rewriting it in a more comprehensible form and style. This may involve writing manuals, directions, installation guides, repair instructions, books, film scripts, training programs, or any number of factual pieces. There is even some commercial work for technical writers in advertising, press relations, and industrial sales. Technical writers use a potent combination of strong writing skills and grounding in at least one technical field, for example, computer science, engineering, medicine, or aerospace.

The other common definition states that technical writers are responsible for writing technical material for others who are versed in this material to read. The medical technical writer might take the results of a number of studies and write a review of the material comparing the studies. The computer science technical writer might help prepare a paper for delivery at a major software conference. The engineering technical writer might produce a document reviewing stress and fatigue studies on a particular kind of steel I beam. Both definitions express the role of a technical writer, and many technical writers do both kinds of jobs.

The very existence of this profession may be a result of advances in technology moving exponentially faster than the pace of human utilization. The tremendous developments in the computer industry in terms of speed of processing argue for someone to help us bridge the gap between what exists and what we can understand based on our own experiences and education. Without the assistance of technical writers, there might be a frightening and divisive gap between science and everyday life.

So we have come to need the services of technical writers; in fact, we rely on them to a great extent. We hear about a new digital camera. We may not entirely understand how it works, but we know that if we acquire it, it will come with instructions to allow us to incorporate it into our lives.

The intensive care nurse on the neonatal ward of a children's hospital places the same trust in the installation and operating instructions that accompany a new infant incubation unit. Although the nurse may appreciate the features and understand the need for them, without a technical manual on how to program, troubleshoot, and operate the system, the equipment would be useless.

There have always been technical specialists who wrote, but with the proliferation of technology, the field has shifted from technical specialists who write to writers who are grounded in technology. A skilled writer with a technical background can be a powerful member of a team developing any kind of structured systems design product that requires written documentation. Of course, end users will need this documentation and the training it provides to use a new system, whatever that system may be. But, increasingly, the technical writer is involved during product development. A good technical communicator can be indispensable in helping to analyze user requirements, clarify the documentation process, and solve increasingly complex communication problems with information systems management staff. The insightful technical writer can help enhance the efficiency of a design.

To fully understand how technical writers can contribute to systems design, a shift in thinking is needed. Technical writers included in a design team early on in planning can help the firm turn out a higher-quality product while reducing time and costs of systems development, testing, revision, and documentation. There are several reasons why a technical writer might make a good designer. Traditionally, it is a writer's skill to determine what a user needs to know and when. This helps the writer to create a logical flow of information. Technical writers can combine this user's perspective with their own experience and ability to emphasize logic, simplicity, usability, and consistency.

The change in role here is dramatic. Rather than functioning solely as the software documenter at the end of a development process, the technical writer now joins the team early on in product development to bring an end-user perspective that may have dramatic implications for product design, development, and features.

Fortunately for those aspiring to be technical writers, this proliferation of technology has not been limited to one or even a few sectors of the economy. For example, the dramatic changes in the pharmaceutical industry as it works overtime to challenge the threats of cancer and heart disease; the computer and software industries and their continued appearance in every aspect of our lives; robotics in manufacturing; dramatic new surgical procedures and techniques and postsurgical care in medicine; and research work in communications, energy, and precision instruments are but a few of the countless developments signaling employment for the technical writer.

Writers document procedures such as how to grow bacteria, build complex viruses, develop artificial insulin, and cleanse cholesterol. Many advances in science, especially biology and chemistry, suggest that these may be promising backgrounds for future technical writers. Robotics will also provide a fruitful proving ground for new advances in engineering and hydraulics. Some of this growth seems to be localized geographically in familiar regions such as California's Silicon Valley, the Pacific Northwest, Atlanta, central Florida, New Jersey, and Washington, D.C.

The growth of technology has led to many new, smaller, start-up organizations, many of which need technical writing expertise but not on a full-time basis. Technical writers who are entrepreneurially inclined might enjoy freelancing for a number of different organizations. What they lack in benefits and stability, they may recover in higher fees and the pleasure of an ever-changing workload.

Technology is complex, and the need for technical writers was born out of that complexity. The technology sector of our economy remains the largest employer, both currently and prospectively, for aspiring technical writers. But life in general has grown increasingly complex, and technical writers can also be found in colleges, universities, and even in advertising agencies. Technical writers can work for book, magazine, and newspaper publishers as well. Some technical writers work for the U.S. Government Printing Office producing brochures and pamphlets that cover many different fields: activities of various government agencies and reports on government work in agriculture, medicine, science, and aerospace.

Some technical writers work in nonscience areas as well. There are technical writers in large insurance companies who explain terms and procedures to field agents, claims adjusters, and others who work for the firm. Technical writers can produce contracts, policies, and procedural manuals for any field from commercial shipping to banking.

In seeking entry into a field that might lead to a technical writing position, look for job descriptions that emphasize work that will provide opportunities to acquire the knowledge base you will need to attain a technical writing position. To better understand the varied duties and responsibilities inherent in a technical writer's job, let's look at the occupation-specific tasks and activities outlined in the *O*NET Dictionary of Occupational Titles* (http://online.onetcenter.org):

Analyze developments in specific field to determine need for revisions in previously published materials and development of new material. Arrange for typing, duplication, and distribution of material. Assist in laying out material for publication. Confer with customer representatives, vendors, plant executives, or publisher to establish technical specifications and to determine subject material to be developed for publication. Draw sketches to illustrate specified materials or assembly sequence. Edit, standardize, or make changes to material prepared by other writers or establishment personnel. Interview production and engineering personnel and read journals and other material to become familiar with product technologies and production methods. Maintain records and files of work and revisions. Observe production, developmental, and experimental activities to determine operating procedure and detail. Organize material and complete writing assignment according to set standards regarding order, clarity, conciseness, style, and terminology. Review manufacturer's and trade catalogs, drawings, and other data relative to operation, maintenance, and service of equipment. Review published materials and recommend revisions or changes in scope, format, content, and methods of reproduction and binding. Select photographs, drawings, sketches, diagrams, and charts to illustrate material. Study drawings, specifications, mockups, and product samples to integrate and delineate technology, operating procedure, and production sequence and detail.

Technical writers emerge from two possible entry-level sites. The college graduate with an English major and sufficient technical background or willingness to acquire such background may begin as a technical writing research assistant or a technician in any of the employment sectors hiring technical writers. The employee would spend this entry-level time acquiring increasingly sophisticated technical information about the organization and its products. Larger firms may contribute substantially to a promising employee with courses, workshops, seminars, and professional conference invitations.

Other entry-level positions are for technicians with an interest in developing writing skills as technical writers. These individuals are most often already employed within an organization and seek either job change or job modification to explore this possibility. In most cases they would be assigned to work closely with an established staff technical writer who would give them research assignments and pieces of writing to edit and use as a training tool to improve the quality of the trainee's writing efforts.

The promotion ladder next moves up to full-fledged technical writer and from there to technical editor. The technical editor assigns tasks, monitors work flow and deadline dates, and has overall responsibility for quality. This individual, as a department head, might also evaluate employees, manage the department budget, make equipment purchases, hire new staff, and participate in other organizational efforts.

The following actual advertisements are illustrative of established technical writing positions and detail not only desired backgrounds and qualifications but also suggest the variety of settings in which technical writing takes place:

Technical Writer. Restaurant industry. Publicly traded full service restaurant company with forty locations and new restaurants opening this year. Responsible for developing, writing, and editing training materials for initiatives and projects; updating all training material; clarifying and reorganizing draft material for content and structure; suggesting ways to present material; ensuring consistency is maintained across documents; developing and maintaining a schedule for all assigned editing and meeting associated deadlines; maintaining and updating the style guide. B.A. required, solid knowledge of Word, familiarity with tools common to tech writers, Quark experience preferred, restaurant experience preferred.

Junior Technical Writer. Leading provider of temp IT professionals. Duties: gather information to produce end-user documentation, carry out technical writing assignments (software user guides, release notes, online help, Web-based documents), and proofread and edit documents. Formal education in technical writing required, some experience preferred.

Environmental Technical Writer. Environmental agency. Acquire and summarize key documents; assist with the preparation of fact sheets, project summaries, testimonials, and case studies; assist in contacting principal investigators receiving grant funding; review material to develop charts, graphs, and other graphics; assist with developing material for website. Requires bachelor's degree and some experience.

Working Conditions

Most technical writers live in or near major metropolitan areas. Jobs are available around the country, but they are concentrated in New York, Chicago, Los Angeles, Boston, Philadelphia, San Francisco, and Washington, D.C.

Working conditions will depend on the industry and type of specialty required. Many technical writers are employed in the software industry, which tends to provide more flexible hours and allow more casual dress, although many hours of overtime may be required as release dates and publishing deadlines approach.

Some technical writers handle pieces of machinery or operate computer programs to determine the best way to explain the procedures. For many other technical writers, their day is sedentary as they sit at a personal computer to produce their written product. Freelance technical writers often work odd hours to fit this work into another full-time work schedule.

The most important aspect of technical writers' working conditions is that they must constantly be learning new technologies and developments in their field of expertise in order to remain attractive to their employer or contractor. Most begin any new project with extensive research, so some of their time is spent on the Internet and in libraries and research facilities. But not all their research is on the Web or with books and manuscripts. They may be called on to do some interviewing as well. Both research activities and interviewing assignments can provide some travel opportunities and variety to the working conditions of a technical writer.

Training and Qualifications

Technical writing positions require at least a four-year degree, and it can take up to six additional years of training or schooling to acquire the specialized knowledge necessary to work in some areas. Students graduating with a degree in English must begin as early as they can to build an area of technical expertise. Choosing a minor in a science or computers is one way to accomplish this.

Effective communication skills are required in this occupation. Many would wrongly assume that this job is solitary or suitable for an introverted person. In fact, as a technical writer you will interact with countless other professionals and will need to be a superb communicator at all levels. The writer must be prepared to extract information from others who use a highly specific and technical vocabulary.

Though technical writers come from any number of educational backgrounds, including English, they share many basic skills. They are required to be logical, disciplined, accurate, and detailed in their writing. They often must thoroughly research their subject matter before beginning to write, and confer early and frequently with other authorities in the field to ensure accuracy and quality of information. They must have strong research skills, and they frequently employ research in their preparation to write. In this preparation, they may encounter technical diagrams, blueprints, schematics, flowcharts, and any number of highly specialized and technical aids, which they must then interpret.

Accuracy and attention to detail are critical. It cannot be stressed enough that "attention to detail" for technical writers is of an entirely different order than our everyday use of that phrase. Some might say it needs to be almost pathological because the detail in technical writing is the essence of the work. Poise under pressure and the ability to work with deadlines make aspects of this job similar to news reporting. Curiosity and aggressiveness about acquiring information suggest that some qualities of a detective would be helpful.

In addition to consultations throughout the writing process with other experts in the field, the technical writer's work is subject to final review by professionals in the subject area. In fact, much technical writing is collaborative, and the technical writer must be comfortable working and creating in a team environment.

The foundation of the technical writer's skill, however, is not just excellent writing, but a thorough grounding in some technical specialty. For this reason, entry-level technical writing positions are a little more scarce than those requiring solid experience. Technical writers sometimes gravitate to this profession after some years of work in a technical specialty. Writing skill can be developed and polished in the general writing assignments that we encounter in the work environment, but technical writing is founded on knowledge and expertise gained through experience. Aspiring technical writers often begin by doing research or working alongside an established technical writer, helping with drafts and editing.

This skill is more than simple translation of the material from technospeak to plain English; it is, in fact, the transformation of material that is too obtuse to be useful into information that can be easily understood and appreciated by the intended audience. So the writing, while crucial, cannot really be separated from the technical skill and grounding in the specialized field. The explosion of information has led the Society for Technical Communications to create a number of Special Interest Groups (SIG). Each SIG is composed of members with common experiences and interests who share their skills and knowledge with each other and with other STC members. A few examples are Canadian Issues, Information Design, and Scientific Communication.

It is certainly understandable in reading about the technical expertise and attention to detail required of a technical writer that some individuals interested in this career may feel that this isn't really writing, but rather some kind of robotic translation. Nothing could be further from the truth. Many current scholars point out that as far back as Geoffrey Chaucer's *A Treatise on the Astrolabe* we have marvelous models for how technical writers can incorporate into their works rhetorical components such as coherent organization, appropriate content, accurate descriptions, personable tone, varied sentence structure, and even humor.

Although even practicing technical writers may find it difficult to inject humor into their writing, it has been argued that the use of humor as part of a technical writing text gives documentation several advantages, including the suggestion that both the writer and designer are genuinely engaged in the subject. That engagement is compelling to the reader and lightens what might otherwise be an overly heavy approach to the subject. There's no question that most documentation is seen as dreary in style and content. The argument here is not for humor for the sake of humor, but rather for humor judiciously used to enhance the documentation. The continuing dialogue on this and other stylistic matters shows there certainly is a place for the thinking, stylistically concerned writer in the field of technical writing.

It will come as no surprise to aspiring technical writers that their command of computer technology must be substantially more than simple word-processing skills. Desktop publishing familiarity would be considered a basic skill, as would some computer graphics, analysis software, spreadsheet capability, and any number of other programs for the manipulation of data. All of these would be helpful to the technical writer and add to a candidate's attractiveness in this market.

The following phrases from recent job descriptions are representative of nearly every ad that was examined, and they highlight the importance of building experience in a range of software applications: "Requires two to four years experience with MS Office." "Must be knowledgeable with all Windows XP applications, i.e., Word, PowerPoint, Excel, Graphics." "Familiarity with HTML a plus." "Working knowledge of database software is required." "Experience with developing Web pages." Knowledge of Visio, Adobe Acrobat, and Photoshop."

Earnings

As of this writing, the average salary range for an entry-level technical writer is $36,300 to $42,500. Be sure to check a website such as salary.com for the most current information available.

How much freelancers earn varies widely and has much to do with their experience, subject matter specialty, and reputation as well as the nature and originator of whatever assignment they are working on. Since they are self-employed, they must provide their own benefits. Many job postings were found on the Web, and some listed the amount that would be paid.

Career Outlook

The outlook for technical writers is excellent. The U.S. Department of Labor, Bureau of Labor Statistics, reports faster than average growth of technical writers due to the proliferation of scientific and technical information and the need to communicate that information.

Approximately fifty thousand people worked as technical writers in the United States in 2003, and that number is projected to grow to sixty-three thousand in the year 2012. The federal government employs a number of these workers. Nongovernment workers are employed in a wide range of industries, and the employment outlook will vary with the industry in which you hope to be employed.

Revolutions in the personal computer market, networking capabilities, and the use of laptops, notebooks, personal digital devices, and other types of equipment all suggest that the need for technical writers in the computer hardware industry will grow. Existing and emerging technologies in several types of software will also provide opportunities for growth in the software industry, traditionally one of the largest sources of employment for technical writers.

The increasing use of online retail trade, especially in the customer service area, provides many job opportunities for technical writers. They assist in developing product information and technical information that is posted on a company's Internet site. This information allows companies to efficiently manage customer relations and improve customer satisfaction. Growth is also projected in the biotechnology industry, which introduces breakthrough processes and products in medicine, agriculture, and the environment.

Some industries do not hold as much promise, however. Be sure to do some basic research on any industry you are considering. A good resource for exploring this subject is the Internet. Simply use your favorite search engine, enter the industry name, and then begin reviewing the many citations. Information will include discussions of short- and long-term industry prospects, including employment trends.

Strategy for Finding the Jobs

By targeting the type of technical writing you want to do, targeting specific industries, and identifying useful resources for job listings, you will find the job search to be easier than you might have originally thought. Read on for more information about how to accomplish each of these tasks.

Target the Type of Technical Writing You Want to Do

Technical writers possess a technical knowledge base in at least one field, so your job search will be affected by the depth of your specialized knowledge at this point. You might already have a solid background in a given field or industry. Perhaps you have a minor in computer information systems and have done an internship with a software manufacturer. In this case, you'll want to network with employers and review the many job listings made available by professional associations such as the Society for Technical Communication (stc.org) and other job sites on the Internet. Some associations allow only members to review job listings. Two examples are the American Medical Writers Association (amwa.org) and the National Association of Science Writers (nasw.org). Nonetheless, their sites provide much useful information.

Target Specific Industries

If you have not yet had an opportunity to build a level of technical expertise, begin your job search by identifying industries that truly interest you. The next few years will be a continuation of your education as you increase your knowledge in a given field, so choose something you can get excited about. Once you identify an industry, begin reviewing entry-level job postings in that field to develop a list of potential employers. If you have the funds, join a professional organization that serves this type of worker. Once you develop a list of employers, contact them and conduct informational interviews with as many as you can. Between your review of the job listings and your networking activity, you will quickly gain an understanding of the job possibilities in your chosen sector of the economy and for the geographic location you are targeting.

Identify Useful Resources

Begin your search for actual job listings for technical writing positions, or positions that will allow you to begin building a technical expertise, by using the Internet. Just a few of the major Internet career sites that will lead you to these types of position advertisements are careerbuilder.com, jobbankusa .com, and monster.com. As you spend more time exploring career sites, it will become easier to find the kind of job description and listing you are looking for.

Possible Employers

As you discovered in previous sections of this chapter, the employment opportunities for technical writers can be found anywhere there is technical information that needs to be relayed to other professionals working in the industry, or where there is information that needs to be simplified for a lay audience. These needs cross nearly every industrial and geographic boundary. Industries needing and hiring technical writers include the following:

- Natural resources and energy
- Construction and related industries
- Industrial materials and components
- Production and manufacturing equipment
- Information and communications
- The consumer economy
- Transportation and travel
- Health care
- Financial services
- Business and professional services
- Public administration

Remember, it is important to build a knowledge base in at least one technical area, so you may want to begin your search for employment by looking for entry-level jobs that will allow you to begin gaining the required expertise.

Listed under each employer category are resources you can use to develop a list of potential employers. Our purpose in listing these resources is simply to help you understand where you can find employers who typically hire in a given industry. Use the information in Chapter 3 to help you identify additional employers who hire technical writers.

Natural Resources and Energy

This industry includes metals and industrial minerals mining, coal mining, crude petroleum and natural gas, petroleum refining, and electricity production and sales; technical writers are needed in each of these areas. For example, companies that operate oil and gas fields use complex equipment and procedures to make oil and gas marketable. Field technicians must have a complete understanding of the equipment and procedures so that they can work efficiently and handle any problems or disasters that may arise.

There is great risk of accident and natural disaster in all aspects of the natural resources and energy field. Mine cave-ins, oil-well blowouts, and underground fires call for quick response and managing highly complex equipment. Instructions and associated visuals must be crystal clear for situations such as these when tension adds to the difficulties. Technical writers help to create manuals and emergency procedure directions so that these high-risk situations can be brought under control in a time- and cost-efficient manner. It is no exaggeration to say that, in these cases, their work can mean the difference between life and death.

Help in Locating These Employers. There are so many hiring companies in this industry that it would be nearly impossible to list them all here. Resources such as *Standard and Poor's Industry Surveys* and *Moody's Industrial Manual* provide lists of companies by type of industry. Use these kinds of references available at your college library to build your list of companies in this industry. Once you identify actual company names using paper-based resources, using the Internet to search for jobs at these companies becomes an easy task to undertake.

Some of the professional organizations that can provide useful information on the petroleum industry include the American Petroleum Institute (api.org), the Coordinating Research Council (crcao.com), the Gas Technology Institute (gastechnology.org), and the Canadian Energy Research Institute (ceri.ca). There are similar professional associations for each of the various natural resources and energy subindustries.

Construction

The construction industry includes private residential, private nonresidential, publicly owned, and international construction firms. The skills of the technical writer are needed here, too. The blending of the aesthetic demands of the architect, the building codes required in a particular locality, cost and energy constraints, and the overriding pressure of labor costs associated with protracted construction schedules all place heavy demands on the technical writer to produce materials that not only synthesize all these competing entities but also provide readable guidelines in the field.

Help in Locating These Employers. Associations and organizations related to this sector of the economy include Associated General Contractors (agc.org), Associated Builders and Contractors (abc.org), and National Association of Homebuilders (nahb.org).

Industrial Materials and Components

When you think about textiles, paper and allied products, chemicals (including drugs and pharmaceuticals), plastics and rubber, metals, general components like valve and pipe fittings, and microelectronic components, you're thinking about activities and products related to the industrial materials and components industry.

Each time a new drug is allowed on the market, specifications on the use of that drug must be provided to doctors, pharmacists, and patients. Dosage requirements, administration protocols, and contraindications for existing conditions or combinations with other drugs require the clearest kind of information. The skill of the technical writer in documenting and presenting this information in an organized and logical way could mean a lifesaving difference for the patient.

Help in Locating These Employers. If you are interested in working as a technical writer in the pharmaceuticals industry, you may want to begin by researching some of the larger companies. Explore Internet sites that provide industry information, or check manuals such as *Ward's Business Directory* or the *Business Rankings Annual* for the names of these companies. Not too long ago an entry-level technical writing position for a large pharmaceutical company was found at careermag.com.

Several organizations that can provide information on pharmaceutical companies and associated jobs include the Pharmaceutical Research and Manufacturers Association (phrma.org), National Association of Pharmaceutical Manufacturers (napmnet.org), and the Nonprescription Drug Manufacturers Association (ndmac.ca).

Associations for just a few of the other products included in this industry are the American Electronics Association, (aeanet.org), the Publishing Mall website (publishingmall.com), Society of the Plastics Industry (socplas .org), Association of American Publishers (publishers.org), and the Valve Manufacturers Association (vma.org).

Production and Manufacturing Equipment

This industry covers a range of manufacturers, including metalworking equipment, production machinery, electrical equipment, environmental technologies and services, aerospace, ship building and repair, industrial and analytical instruments, and photographic equipment and supplies.

If we look more closely at the aerospace industry, we find that it includes aircraft, missiles, and space-launch vehicle production and manufacturing. If you are interested in being involved in technical writing somehow associated with this industry, employers continue to hire technical writers.

Help in Locating These Employers. You could begin your search for employment by finding out which employers manufacture equipment needed to keep space-launch programs operational. Most states' manufacturing activity is summarized in the *Manufacturers Directory*, which is available at many public libraries and college libraries. These directories list manufacturers by their Standard Industrial Classification (SIC) code. For each manufacturer listed, you will usually find contact information (address and phone number), a summary of products, sales information, company officers, and number of employees.

If you are interested in finding out more about employment in the aerospace industry, the Aerospace Industries Association (aia-aerospace.org) can provide information, as can the General Aviation Manufacturers Association (generalaviation.org).

Information and Communications

When you think about printing and publishing, information services, computer equipment, computer software and networking, telecommunications services, telecommunications and navigation equipment, and entertainment and electronics, you are thinking about the information and communications industry.

Many technical writers are employed in this sector of the economy, especially in computer software and networking. One dynamic segment of this industry is CAD/CAM/CAE or computer-aided design, computer-aided manufacturing, and computer-aided engineering. Engineers, designers, and draftspeople all use these types of software and, as new products come onto the market, technical writers must create new instruction manuals to help users effectively incorporate these tools into their work.

Help in Locating These Employers. There are many large as well as small start-up companies that offer employment prospects. The Internet is really the best place to look for industry information, employer names, and job listings. Use any of the major sites (careerbuilder.com, jobbank-usa.com, or monster.com), and begin exploring. And you should plan to submit your résumé via the Internet when seeking a job in the information and communications industry.

A comprehensive website that contains information and related links, and that serves as a reference resource for corporate IT, computer software, computers, and communications is that of the Computer Information Center (compinfo.co.uk/index.htm). Some industry-specific organizations include the Software and Information Industry Association (siia.net) and the Electronic Industries Alliance (eia.org).

Consumer Economy

The consumer economy provides many opportunities to the aspiring technical writer. Wholesaling and retailing of food and beverages, apparel, motor vehicles, household furniture and appliances, and sporting and athletic goods are all a part of this sector of the economy. Nearly every item sold, no matter how simple or complex, is accompanied by a set of user instructions. If you want to sync podcasts to your iPod, you want to be sure that you have set it up correctly to hear all the shows that interest you. So you get out the instruction manual. You find the instructions easy to understand and, in just a few minutes, you've subscribed to lots of free radio shows. Say thanks to the technical writer!

Help in Locating These Employers. There are a myriad of both employers and professional associations connected with the consumer economy. You may be especially interested in one type of product or activity, so let your search begin on the Internet. If bicycling is an interest, then try the Bicycle Helmet Manufacturers' Association (helmets.org/phma.htm); if it's sewing, how about the American Textile Machinery Association (atmanet.org); or if it's cars, how about the Automotive Industry Action Group (aiag.org); you get the idea.

Or you can use the *Encyclopedia of Associations* to locate related professional organizations. Each association will tell you whether it includes job listings on its website or in its newsletter and can advise you on the best sources for additional job listings. Don't hesitate to check their websites for other valuable career information.

Transportation

Transportation includes airlines, railroads, trucking, water transportation, and domestic shipping. Each of these sectors uses complex computerized information systems tailored for its specific use, and technical writers are needed to explain the mechanics of these systems. One of the largest and most complex computerized information systems in place today is the airline reservation system. Computer programmers, computer operators, system managers, airline executives, reservations operators, and travel agencies are all linked together, and each must understand how to use this system. Translations from technical to lay terms are needed when different kinds of system users interact.

Help in Locating These Employers. There are many well-known employers in the transportation industry, and each uses information systems, equipment, and procedures that need to be clearly explained to employees. If you are interested in working in this industry, develop your list by reviewing *Moody's Transportation Manual* at your college or local public library.

Some of the professional associations related to the transportation and travel industry include the Air Transport Association of America (airlines.org), Association of American Railroads (aar.org), American Trucking Associations (truckline.com), and the Lake Carriers Association (lcaships.com).

Health Care

The quality of health care and the way it is delivered in the United States is in the forefront of the news. If you want to be employed in this ever-changing industry, the industrial groups to consider are health and medical services and medical and dental instruments and supplies.

Caring for aging parents using currently available health-care options is one topic receiving a lot of press. Understanding the options—home care, congregate housing, assisted living, continuing-care facilities, and nursing homes—and associated costs is of great import to today's families. The skill of the technical writer is used to document and present this information. Decisions are often made in a time of crisis. An organized, logical, and clear explanation to consumers who will be placing parents in these facilities could mean a real difference in the quality of life for all those involved.

Help in Locating These Employers. If you are interested in working as a technical writer in the health-care industry, you may want to begin your search by going online to find current information on the industry, companies, and associations as well as links to actual job listings. For example, searching the Internet by entering the words "healthcare industry association" will bring up the Canadian Healthcare Information Technology Trade Association's name (chitta.ca) and a number of other sites you can explore.

Several organizations that can provide information on health care include the Medical Device Manufacturers Association (medicaldevices.org), National

Association for Home Care (nahc.org), and the National Association for Healthcare Quality (nahq.org).

Financial and Business Services

You will find commercial banking, international commercial banking, savings institutions, mutual fund companies, securities firms, commodities futures trading companies, and insurance companies in the financial and business services industry. As this industry has grown more complex, its documentation has grown equally complicated, with some surprising results. Consumers, angry about their inability to understand the complexities of legal documents used by these industries, have frequently sued and won court cases over issues of obscure language. Technical writers have been asked to replicate the essence of these complex agreements for financial services in user-friendly language that still conveys all the required legal points of culpability, responsibility, and ownership.

Help in Locating These Employers. Some resources that can be used to generate lists of potential employers include the *National Credit Union Administration Directory*, *Directory of Bond Agents*, *Security Dealers of North America*, and *Best's Insurance Reports*.

Many professional associations are in place for this industry. Just a few of the larger associations include the American Bankers Association (aba.com), Futures Industry Association (futuresindustry.org), National Association of Mutual Insurance Companies (namic.org), and the Insurance Industry Internet Network (iiin.com).

Professional and Business Services

Professional and business services include equipment leasing, accounting, auditing, bookkeeping, advertising, legal services, management, consulting, and public relations. Business associations, professional organizations, and labor organizations are also included in this category.

One of the great success stories of American business has been the restaurant franchise. Many enterprising businesspeople have become millionaires through buying and successfully managing a branch of a national restaurant chain such as Pizza Hut, McDonald's, Burger King, and Hardees. To ensure consistent quality of its products, each of these chains provides every owner with a specification document for each product it sells. If the franchisee can duplicate that product according to these specifications (written by the technical writing staff), they may buy locally. If a local vendor cannot meet these exacting specifications, the franchisee must purchase from the franchise owner. The specifications for McDonald's sesame seed buns even document the density of sesame seed coverage!

Help in Locating These Employers. As you begin to develop a list of potential employers to contact, some references to check include *Who Audits America, Standard Directory of Advertising Agencies, Directory of Management Consultants, Consultants and Consulting Organizations Directory, O'Dwyer's Directory of Corporate Communications,* and *O'Dwyer's Directory of Public Relations Firms.* There are many industry-specific career guides that also list specific company names.

You can contact the American Association of Advertising Agencies (aaaa.org), American Bar Association (abanet.org), American Institute of Certified Public Accountants (aicpa.org), Institute of Management Consultants (imcusa.org), and the Public Relations Society of America (prsa.org) to get more specific information on technical writing and other career opportunities available with that type of employer.

Federal Government

The procedures for shredding and destruction of classified documents, the safe storage procedures for confidential material, the arming of a security system on a naval base, the fire-control trajectory instructions for a shipboard missile assembly, and directions for assembling and heating field rations are just some of the countless ways in which technical writers provide needed skills in the federal government.

Help in Locating These Employers. Many federal agencies employ technical writers; a few of the largest agencies include the Department of the Interior, Department of Agriculture, National Aeronautics and Space Administration, Department of Defense, Nuclear Regulatory Commission, Environmental Protection Agency, National Institutes of Health, Centers for Disease Control, and the Department of Energy. Most of these agencies operate their own personnel/human resources function, so contacting them directly is a good way to begin. A place to start looking for actual job listings is on the U.S. government's website, usajobs.opm.gov. This site explains the federal employment process and lets you look at current job openings, get general information on federal agencies, and submit an online application.

If you select the option "Search Jobs" and then do a keyword search using "technical writer," a list of open positions will be generated. Select any of the entries and a detailed job description will be provided, including information on whom to contact for more information and how to apply for the specific position.

State and Local Government

State and local governments continue to be impacted by a variety of federal legislation in every area of government. Social services, wetlands conservation, schools, hospitals, and taxes have all become increasingly complex and the subject of intense public scrutiny and emotion. In every case and at every level, directives and policies must be reinterpreted and tailored to the region, locality, or government level involved. This is the job of the technical writer.

Help in Locating These Employers. Some state and local governments provide both entry-level positions that can help you build your technical knowledge base and actual technical writing jobs. Start by contacting the state or city human resources department in the geographic area where you would like to work. Talk with someone there about departments and offices that hire technical writers. Many state and local government jobs are listed in each state's larger newspapers, and websites contain job listings. Use your favorite search engine and enter "State of (put state name here)." You will find references to state departments; look for Employment, Personnel, or Human Resources, then look for job listings, opportunities, and so on. You will also find application procedures and contact names, and some sites will allow you to apply online. Don't hesitate to directly contact government units that you discover have a need for technical writing skills. Be proactive and let the directors of those government units know you have skills they can put to use.

Possible Job Titles

Technical writing jobs are usually advertised as such, but you will also see:

Technical communicator
Medical writer
Technical editor
Publications specialist
Science writer
Usability specialist
Documentation manager
Information developer

Documentation specialist
Technical translator

As you begin to consider entry-level jobs that could be used to gain expertise in a specific industry or discipline, the range of job titles to consider expands. Look for job titles that might include:

Media associate
Marketing associate
Proposal writer
Associate editor
Editorial assistant
Copywriter
Museum assistant
Research assistant
Field technician
Lab technician
Designer
Computer programmer
Systems analyst
Reporter

Related Occupations

There are three often-mentioned job titles that relate to technical writing: researcher, science journalist, and public information writer. A brief description of each follows.

Researchers conduct studies and gather verbal or statistical information. They then analyze the data and prepare reports to describe their findings. Researchers work in nearly any discipline you can imagine, including law, medicine, politics, genetic engineering, physics, animal care, food science, agronomy, geology, meteorology, soils, oceanography, and psychology.

Science journalists translate technical information into a public interest format and relate that information via newspaper and magazine articles, press releases, radio and TV scripts, trade books, textbooks, information booklets, and encyclopedia entries.

Public information writers usually work for high-technology industries, public research agencies, or colleges and universities. These writers help the outside world understand research efforts going on within their organization.

They may use the written word, photographs, videotapes, or audiotapes to convey their message to various audiences, including chief executive officers, members of the general public, alumni, or representatives from news organizations.

Professional Associations for Technical Writers

Many associations can provide information valuable to your job search in technical writing, but there are a few that you especially should consider contacting. Find out about membership benefits as you request more general information from the group. Joining any of these associations will increase your knowledge of current industry trends and issues, all of which affect hiring prospects.

American Medical Writers Association
9650 Rockville Pike
Bethesda, MD 20814
amwa.org
Members/Purpose: Medical writers, editors, audiovisualists, public
   relations, and pharmaceutical personnel; publishers; and others
   concerned with communication in medicine and allied sciences
Training: Hosts conferences
Journals/Publications: Journal, membership directory, freelance directory
Job Listings: Members can access job postings online

Canadian Science Writers Association
P.O. Box 75, Station A
Toronto, ON
M5W 1A2
sciencewriters.ca
Members/Purpose: Media professionals, communications officers in science
   and technology institutions, technical writers, and educators
Training: Hosts annual conference
Job Listings: Online job board lists open positions

Construction Writers Association
P.O. Box 5586
Buffalo Grove, IL 60089
constructionwriters.org

Members/Purpose: Writers and editors for media, public relations, and advertising in the construction field

Journal/Publication: Newsletter

Job Listings: Help-wanted tab on website shows current openings

National Association of Science Writers

P.O. Box 890

Hedgesville, WV 25427

nasw.org

Members/Purpose: Writers and editors engaged in the preparation and interpretation of science news for the public

Journal/Publication: *Science Writers* quarterly review

New York Financial Writers Association

P.O. Box 338

Ridgewood, NJ 07451-0338

nyfwa.org

Members/Purpose: Financial and business editors and writers whose publications are located in metropolitan New York

Journal/Publication: Directory

Job Listings: Listings are available to members only

Society for Technical Communication

901 N. Stuart St., Suite 904

Arlington, VA 22203-1854

stc.org

Members/Purpose: Technical writers and editors, content developers, documentation specialists, technical illustrators, instructional designers, academics, information architects, usability and human factors professionals, visual designers, Web designers and developers, and translators dedicated to advancing the arts and sciences of technical communication

Training: Society offers seminars, lectures, workshops, international symposia, and an annual conference to keep technical communicators informed of latest techniques and methods in communication

Journals/Publications: *Intercom Online, TechComm, Proceedings*

Job Listings: Online job listings posted in the Career Center

Additional Resources

ABI/Inform on Disk. CD-ROM and online. Ann Arbor, MI: UMI-Data Courier, Inc.

American Bar Association Member Directory. Chicago: American Bar Association, 2004.

America's Corporate Families. Bethlehem, PA: Dun and Bradstreet Information Services, 2005.

ARTSearch. New York: Theatre Communications Group, 2005.

Audio Video Market Place. Medford, NJ: Information Today, 2005.

Best's Insurance Reports. Oldwick, NJ: A. M. Best Co., 2002.

Bowling, Anne. *2005 Novel and Short Story Writer's Market.* Cincinnati: Writer's Digest Books, 2004.

Burrelle's Media Directory. Livingston, NJ: Burrelle's Media Directories, 2005.

Business Rankings Annual. Detroit: Thomson Gale, 2006.

The Career Guide: Dun's Employment Opportunities Directory. Parsippany, NJ: Dun's Marketing Service.

Careers in Communications. Chicago: McGraw-Hill, 2004.

Careers in Health Care. Chicago: McGraw-Hill, 2005.

Careers in Journalism. Chicago: McGraw-Hill, 2005.

Careers in Writing. Lincolnwood, IL: McGraw-Hill, 2000.

The Chronicle of Higher Education. Washington, DC: The Chronicle of Higher Education, 2005.

Consultants and Consulting Organizations Directory. Detroit: Thomson Gale, 2005.

County Directory. Bethesda, MD: Carroll Publishing, 2005.

Credit Unions Online Job Center (creditunionsonline.com). Albuquerque: CommonBond Communications, Inc., 2005.

Current Jobs for Graduates. Falls Church, VA: Foster Opportunities, Inc., 2005.

Current Jobs in Writing, Editing and Communications. Falls Church, VA: Foster Opportunities, Inc., 2005.

Dialing for Jobs: Using the Phone in the Job Search. DVD or VHS. Indianapolis: JIST Works, Inc., 2000.

Directory of City Policy Officials and Resource Guide. Washington, DC: National League of Cities, 2005.

Directory of Management Consultants. Peterborough, NH: Kennedy Information, 2002.

DISCOVER Career Guidance and Information System CD-ROM. Iowa City, IA: American College Testing, 2005.

Encyclopedia of Associations: Regional, State, and Local Organizations. Detroit: Thomson Gale, 2000.

Environmental Opportunities. Keene, NH: Environmental Studies Department, Antioch/New England Graduate School, 2005.

Equal Employment Opportunity Bimonthly. Northbrook, IL: CRS Recruitment Publications/CASS Communications, Inc., 2005.

Federal Career Opportunities. New York: Gordon Press Publishers, 2005.

Federal Jobs Digest. Washington, DC: Breakthrough Publications, Inc., 2005.

Folio: The Magazine for Magazine Management. Stamford, CT: Six River Bend Center, 2005.

Foundation Grants to Individuals Online (http://gtionline.fndcenter.org). New York: The Foundation Center, 2005.

Gale Directory of Publications and Broadcast Media. Detroit: Thomson Gale, 2003.

Graduate Management Admission Test. McLean, VA: Graduate Management Admission Council, 2005.

Graduate Record Examinations. Princeton, NJ: Graduate Record Examinations Board Educational Testing Services, 2005.

The Handbook of Private Schools. Boston: Porter Sargent Staff, 2004.

Harrington-O'Shea Career Decision Making System CD-ROM. Circle Pines, MN: American Guidance Service, 2005.

Hoover's Handbook of American Business. Austin, TX: Hoover's Inc., 2004.

Hunt, Kimberly (editor). *Encyclopedia of Associations: National Organizations of the U.S.* Farmington Hills, MI: Thomson Gale, 2004.

Independent School Magazine. Washington, DC: National Association of Independent Schools, 2005.

Index of Majors and Graduate Degrees 2003. New York: College Board Publications, 2002.

Infotrac CD-ROM Business and Index. CD-ROM. Farmington Hills, MI: Thomson Gale, 2005.

The International Educator Online (tieonline.com). Cummaquid, MA: The International Educator, 2004.

Job Bank series. Holbrook, MA: Bob Adams, Inc.

Lauber, Daniel. *Government Job Finder: Where the Jobs Are in Local, State, and Federal Government.* River Forest, IL: Planning/Communications, 2006.

Lauber, Daniel. *Non-Profits Job Finder.* River Forest, IL: Planning/Communications, 2006.

Municipal Executive Directory. Washington, DC: Carroll Publishing Co., 2005.

Myers-Briggs Type Indicator. Mountain View, CA: CPP, Inc., 2004.

National Directory of Arts Internships. Los Angeles: National Network for Artist Placement, 2005.

The National JobBank. Buffalo, NY: Advanced Educational Products, Inc., 2006.

National Teacher Exam. Princeton, NJ: Educational Testing Service, 2005.

National Trade and Professional Associations of the United States. Washington, DC: Columbia Books Inc., 2005.

The Newspaper Guild (newsguild.org).

Occupational Outlook Handbook. Washington, DC: U.S. Department of Labor Bureau of Labor Statistics, 2006.

O'Dwyer's Directory of Public Relations Firms. New York: J. R. O'Dwyer Co. Inc., 2005.

Opportunities in Banking Careers. Lincolnwood, IL: McGraw-Hill, 2000.

Opportunities in Direct Marketing Careers. Lincolnwood, IL: McGraw-Hill, 2001.

Opportunities in Government Careers. Lincolnwood, IL: McGraw-Hill, 2001.

Opportunities in Journalism Careers. Lincolnwood, IL: McGraw-Hill, 2001.

Opportunities in Psychology Careers. Lincolnwood, IL:, McGraw-Hill, 2001.

Opportunities in Publishing Careers. Lincolnwood, IL: McGraw-Hill, 2000.

Opportunities in Television and Video Careers. Chicago: McGraw-Hill, 2003.

Overseas Employment Opportunities for Educators. Alexandria, VA: DIANE Publishing Co., 2000.

Patterson's American Education. Chester, PA: Educational Directories, 2004.

Patterson's Elementary Education. Chester, PA: Educational Directories, 2003.

Peterson's Guide to Four-Year Colleges. Lawrenceville, NJ: Peterson's Guides, 2005.

Poet's Market. Cincinnati: Writer's Digest Books, 2005.

Publishers Weekly. New York: Publisher's Weekly, 2005.

Savageau, David. *Places Rated Almanac.* Special millennium edition. Foster City, CA: IDG Books Worldwide, 2000.

Schools Abroad of Interest to Americans. Boston: Porter Sargent Publishers, 2005.

SIGI PLUS CD-ROM. Princeton, NJ.

Skills Identification: Discovering Your Skills. DVD and VHS. Indianapolis: JIST Works, Inc., 2000.

Song Writer's Market. Cincinnati: Writer's Digest Books, 2004.

Sports Marketplace. Princeton, NJ: Sportsguide, 2004.

Standard and Poor's Industry Surveys. New York: Standard and Poor's Corp., 2005.

Standard and Poor's Register of Corporations. New York: Standard and Poor's Corp., 2005.

Standard and Poor's Security Dealers of North America. Columbus, OH: McGraw-Hill, 2002.

Standard Directory of Advertising Agencies. New Providence, NJ: National Register Publishing, 2001.

Strong Interest Inventory. Mountain View, CA: CPP, Inc., 2004.

The Tough New Labor Market and What It Takes to Succeed. DVD and VHS. Indianapolis, IN: JIST Works, Inc., 2000.

Upper Valley Teacher Institute. Lebanon, NH. uvti.org.

U.S. News and World Report. Washington, DC. usnews.com/usnews/home.htm.

Who Audits America. Menlo Park, CA: Data Financial Press, 2005.

World Chamber of Commerce Directory. Loveland, CO: World Chamber of Commerce Directory, 2005.

Writer's Market. Cincinnati: Writer's Digest Books, 2005.

Y National Vacancy List Online. ymca.net/employment/ymca_recruiting/jobright.htm. Chicago: YMCA of the USA.

Index